FOOTPRINT READING LIBRARY
COLLECTION
LEVEL 2

Rob Waring, *Series Editor*

Australia • Brazil • Japan • Korea • Mexico • Singapore • Spain • United Kingdom • United States

HEINLE
CENGAGE Learning

Footprint Reading Library Collection: Level 2
Series Editor: Rob Waring

Publisher: *Sherrise Roehr*
Associate Development Editor: *Catherine McCue*
Editorial Assistant: *Heidi North*
Assistant Editor: *Marissa Petrarca*
Director of Marketing: *Jim McDonough*
Product Marketing Manager: *Katie Kelley*
Content Project Manager: *Jin Hock Tan*
Print Buyer: *Susan Carroll*

Copyright © 2010 Heinle, Cengage Learning.

ALL RIGHTS RESERVED. No part of this work covered by the copyright herein may be reproduced, transmitted, stored or used in any form or by any means graphic, electronic, or mechanical, including but not limited to photocopying, recording, scanning, digitizing, taping, Web distribution, information networks, or information storage and retrieval systems, except as permitted under Section 107 or 108 of the 1976 United States Copyright Act, without the prior written permission of the publisher.

> For permission to use material from this text or product, submit all requests online at
> **www.cengage.com/permissions**
>
> Further permissions questions can be emailed to
> **permissionrequest@cengage.com**

Library of Congress Control Number: 2006908272
ISBN 13: 978-1-4240-4514-3
ISBN 10: 1-4240-4514-2

Heinle
20 Channel Center Street
Boston, Massachusetts 02210
USA

Cengage Learning is a leading provider of customized learning solutions with office locations around the globe, including Singapore, the United Kingdom, Australia, Mexico, Brazil, and Japan. Locate our local office at: **international.cengage.com/region**

Cengage Learning products are represented in Canada by Nelson Education, Ltd.

Visit Heinle online at **elt.heinle.com**
Visit our corporate website at **www.cengage.com**

Printed in the United States of America.

1 2 3 4 5 6 7 8 9 10 — 13 12 11 10 09

Contents

Incredible Animals

Farley the Red Panda A1

Gorilla Watching Tours B1

Puffin Rescue! C1

Fascinating Places

A Disappearing World D1

The Knife Markets of Sanaa E1

A Special Kind of Neighborhood... F1

Remarkable People

The Last of the Cheju Divers G1

Peruvian Weavers H1

Taiko Master I1

Contents (continued)

Exciting Activities

Cheese-Rolling Races J1

Making a Thai Boxing Champion K1

Water Sports Adventure L1

Amazing Science

Dinosaur Search M1

The Memory Man N1

Wild Animal Trackers... O1

Farley the Red Panda

Rob Waring, *Series Editor*

Australia • Brazil • Japan • Korea • Mexico • Singapore • Spain • United Kingdom • United States

Words to Know

This story is set in the United States (U.S.). It happens in San Diego, California, and in a city called Syracuse [sirəkyus] in the state of New York.

 At the Zoo. Read the paragraph. Then complete the sentences with the underlined words.

This story begins at the San Diego Zoo. There are many animals that people can see at the zoo. However, this story is about a special red panda named Farley [fɑrli]. When Farley was born at the zoo, the zookeepers took him to be with other young animals at the nursery. There, Farley was raised by hand. Human beings, or people, gave him food and helped him from the time he was very young.

1. _____ are the people who care for animals at a zoo.
2. A _____ is a place for very young animals or children.
3. A _____ is a place where animals are kept and people go to look at them.
4. An animal that is _____ is cared for by people, not other animals.
5. A _____ is an animal that is slightly larger than a cat.

A Red Panda

B **Animal Hospital.** Here are some words you will find in the story. Match each word with the correct definition.

1. hospital _____
2. sick _____
3. medicine _____
4. X-ray _____
5. injection _____
6. tube feed _____

a. something that is put into the body with a needle
b. a special photograph that shows inside of the body
c. a substance that makes people healthy when they are unwell
d. not healthy; unwell
e. give food through a tube
f. a place to take unhealthy people or animals for help

An Animal Hospital

Meet Farley. Farley is more than just a lovable red panda. He's also a fighter! Farley was born at the San Diego Zoo. He was his mother's first baby. Unfortunately, she wasn't able to take care of him when he was born. Zookeepers found him when he was only a few hours old. He was cold, **dirty**,[1] hungry, and alone.

The zookeepers were very worried about Farley, so they took him to the nursery at the zoo. One of the zookeepers describes his condition upon arrival. "When we first got a look at Farley, we were mostly concerned about two things: his early poor **nutrition**[2]—he had not been fed by the mother— and the fact that he was hypothermic, or had a low body **temperature**."[3]

It was clear to everyone that Farley was in trouble.

---

[1] **dirty:** not clean
[2] **nutrition:** the foods that are taken into the body and their effects on health
[3] **temperature:** how hot or cold something is

 CD 1, Track 01

At the time, nursery workers didn't have much experience raising red pandas by hand. Farley was their first. However, they soon discovered how to do it successfully.

One nursery worker talked about Farley's time in the nursery. According to her, it was difficult at first—and a little **nerve-wracking**![4] But soon everyone in the nursery was pleased with Farley's improved health. Everything seemed to be going very well for him. But unfortunately Farley's problems weren't over yet.

---

[4]**nerve-wracking:** difficult to do and causing worry for the people involved

When he was only three weeks old, Farley stopped eating as much as he usually did. He couldn't **breathe**[5] very easily, either. The zookeepers took him to the zoo's hospital immediately. Farley had a very bad infection in his body and he was very sick. He was fighting for his life! For some time, it was uncertain if Farley would live or die.

---

[5]**breathe:** take air into the body

Infer Meaning

What does the word 'infection' mean? Look at the words around it on page A8. Then, write a definition for the word. Check your definition with your teacher or a dictionary.

Farley had to have many weeks of strong medicines and tube feedings. The nursery workers visited Farley every day. With the medicine and lots of care, he slowly got better. After he was in the hospital for a while, the zookeepers began to wonder: is Farley happy? Will all the hospital treatments affect him? After all of this, what kind of character will the little red panda have?

"We kept thinking, what's he going to be like?" reports zookeeper Janet Hawes. "The injections, the tube feedings, the X-rays, the hospital visits … " In the end, they were very pleased with the results. "What came out was just this darling little guy—he was a **doll**!"[6]

---

[6]**doll:** lovable; happy and friendly

After his long stay in the hospital, Farley was finally well enough to move back to his home at the nursery. That's where he's now working on taking his next step—learning to do the things that young red pandas do. One of the nursery workers reports, "The stage we're in right now is just to try to get him to be a better **climber**.[7] He's doing really well **exploring**."[8]

However, it seems Farley's travels aren't over. He has another surprise coming up!

---

[7]**climb:** use the legs, or legs and hands, to move the body up or down on something
[8]**explore:** go around and look for new things

Farley is now going to travel across the country to another zoo in Syracuse, New York. "Good morning, Farley!" says Janet Hawes as she walks into Farley's room. "Today's the big day. How are you feeling?"

Janet and the other zookeepers are a little sad, but they know that he has to go. "Although we'll be very sad to say goodbye to Farley," she says, "he's been just a great, great experience for us. We know he needs more now than we can give him."

What does Farley need? He needs to be around other red pandas. And at the Syracuse Zoo, Farley can finally get what he needs.

Meet Banshee. Banshee is another red panda. He was raised by hand in the Syracuse Zoo. He's about three weeks younger than Farley. According to zookeepers, it's very important for young red pandas to have other red pandas around them. "It's very important for red pandas as youngsters to have **playmates**[9] so that they don't **bond**[10] so completely with human beings," one zookeeper explains.

The zookeepers at Farley's new home in Syracuse are happy. They feel the new relationship between the two red pandas is a success. One of them explains, "As you can see, they're really active and they really like each other's company. And they like to play and sleep together now."

---

[9] **playmate:** a partner that one plays with often
[10] **bond:** form a relationship with someone or something

Back at the San Diego Zoo, Janet Hawes still remembers Farley and how special he was. She explains that Farley was special because he was such a fighter. He fought very hard to live and this fight helped to form his character.

For Janet, Farley was surprisingly friendly and loving, despite the difficult time he had in the beginning. Farley never stopped trying, even though things were very difficult. Janet seems very pleased by what a wonderful animal Farley has become. In fact, she thinks Farley the red panda is a really **'great guy'**![11]

---

[11]**great guy:** friendly term for a good or likeable person

Summarize

Imagine that you are a newspaper or radio reporter. Write or tell Farley's story. Include the following information:

1. How did he start his life?
2. What happened when he got sick?
3. Where is he now?

After You Read

1. On page A4, the word 'fighter' describes an animal that:
   A. is in trouble
   B. tries hard to succeed
   C. is dangerous
   D. argues often

2. Which was NOT one of Farley's problems when he was found?
   A. poor nutrition
   B. hypothermia
   C. hunger
   D. too hot

3. Why was it nerve-wracking for the nursery workers at first?
   A. They had never seen a red panda.
   B. Farley was too small.
   C. They had never raised a red panda by hand.
   D. Farley didn't like to eat.

4. When he was _____ one month old, Farley got a bad infection.
   A. less than
   B. already
   C. over
   D. more than

5. On page A11, 'we' in paragraph two refers to:
   A. the zoo visitors
   B. the red pandas
   C. the zookeepers and nursery workers
   D. Janet Hawes

6. Janet Hawes thinks that Farley is:
   A. unhappy about the treatment
   B. a sweet, friendly animal
   C. very disagreeable
   D. too afraid to be nice

7. Which is a good heading for page A12?
   A. No More Surprises for Farley
   B. Farley Dislikes Exploring
   C. Farley is a Great Climber
   D. More Travels for Farley

8. What happens to Farley?
   A. He moves from San Diego to Syracuse.
   B. He goes to live with other red pandas.
   C. He moves to a new zoo.
   D. all of the above

9. In paragraph 1 on page A15, 'big' means:
   A. important
   B. active
   C. large
   D. real

10. How does Janet feel about saying goodbye to Farley?
   A. unhappy and worried
   B. afraid and worried
   C. sad and happy
   D. afraid and happy

11. Red pandas _____ bond too much with humans.
   A. can't
   B. must not
   C. won't
   D. must

12. What is the main lesson of this story?
   A. Fighting for success builds character.
   B. Pandas like being alone.
   C. Difficult times are impossible.
   D. Red pandas are just like people.

Jobs in Animal Care

Do you love animals? Do you think people must help and protect animals just like humans? Do you want to spend your days helping animals? If you answered 'yes' to any of these questions, maybe you should consider a job in animal care!

ANIMAL RIGHTS OFFICER:

Animal rights officers make sure that people treat animals properly. They visit homes, places where animals are bought and sold, zoos, and animal hospitals. They check to make sure that the places are clean, that the animals are getting proper nutrition, and that they have enough space to climb around and explore. Sometimes an animal rights officer will appear in court to protect the rights of an animal.

Animal Control Officers Help Animals in Danger

A Small Animal Doctor

ANIMAL CONTROL OFFICER:

To be an animal control officer, you must be in very good health because the job is an active one. Sometimes it involves getting animals out of dangerous situations, which can be nerve-wracking. For example, it's not always easy to get a cat down from a tree. Other times, animal control officers must take a sick animal to the hospital for treatment. These animals are often in great pain, and are afraid and difficult to control.

ANIMAL DOCTOR:

An animal doctor is called a 'veterinarian.' Some veterinarians work for zoos or animal hospitals. Others, often called 'small animal doctors,' treat smaller animals like dogs and cats. Many have their own private offices. Veterinarians do most of the same things doctors do. They take the animal's temperature, give injections, and take X-rays. They also decide what kind of medicine a sick animal may need. If an animal weighs too little, the doctor may use a feeding tube to make sure it gets enough nutrition. It takes six to seven years of higher education to become a doctor of veterinary medicine.

CD 1, Track 02

Word Count: 316
Time: _____

Vocabulary List

bond (A: 16)
breathe (A: 8)
climber (A: 12)
dirty (A: 4)
doll (A: 11)
explore (A: 12)
great guy (A: 18)
hospital (A: 3, 8, 11, 12)
injection (A: 3, 11)
medicine (A: 3, 11)
nerve-wracking (A: 7)
nursery (A: 2, 4, 7, 11, 12)
nutrition (A: 4)
playmate (A: 16)
raise by hand (A: 2, 16)
red panda (A: 2, 4, 7, 11, 12, 15, 16, 18)
sick (A: 3, 8, 19)
temperature (A: 4)
tube feed (A: 3, 11)
X-ray (A: 3, 11)
zoo (A: 2, 4, 8, 15, 16, 18)
zookeeper (A: 2, 4, 8, 11, 15, 16)

Gorilla Watching Tours

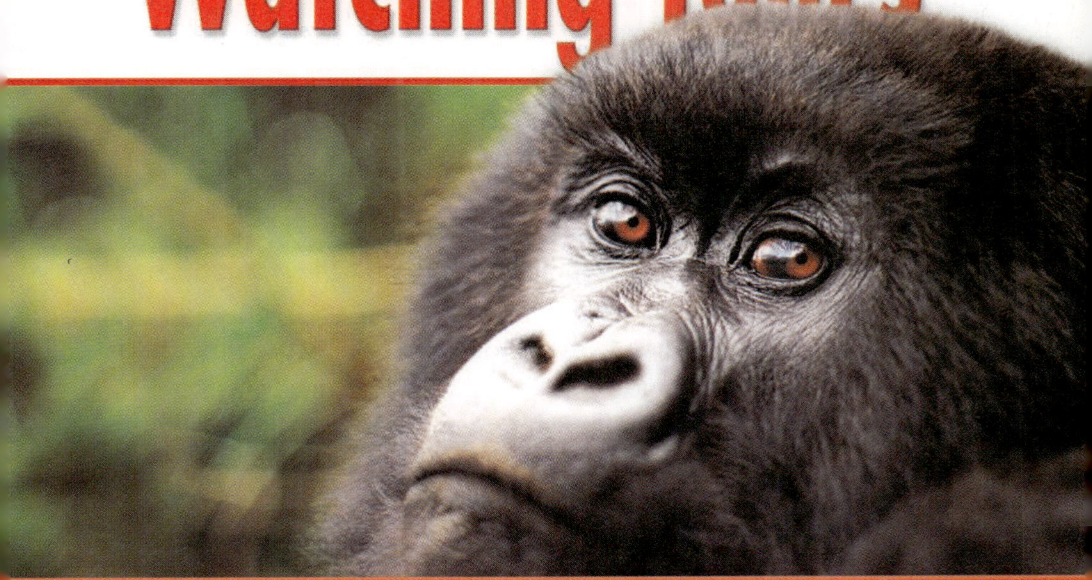

Rob Waring, *Series Editor*

Australia • Brazil • Japan • Korea • Mexico • Singapore • Spain • United Kingdom • United States

B1

Words to Know

This story is set in Africa. It happens in Uganda, [yugændə] in the Bwindi Impenetrable [bwɪndi ɪmpɛnɪtrəbəl] National Park.

A An Unusual Type of Tour.
Read the paragraph. Then match each word with the correct definition.

The Bwindi Impenetrable National Park is well-known for being the home of the mountain gorilla. Ecologists often go there to study the gorillas. However, recently many tourists have also come to the area. They pay guides to go with them into the forest. They want to watch gorillas in their natural environment. The money from these gorilla watching tours helps to keep the gorillas safe. It helps to pay for the conservation of these interesting animals.

1. national park __a__
2. gorilla __f__
3. ecologist __g__
4. tourist __c__
5. guide __d__
6. forest __b__
7. conservation __e__

a. the protection of plants, animals, or natural areas
b. a large area with many trees
c. a visitor who travels for fun
d. a person whose job is showing places to visitors
e. a special area where nature is protected
f. a large animal that lives in Africa
g. a person who studies the relationship between living things and their environments

B **Gorilla Facts.** Read the facts about gorillas. Then write the correct underlined word or phrase next to each definition.

A gorilla is a kind of ape. Gorillas live in groups, or families, like human beings. The leader of each group or family of gorillas is a large male gorilla, called a silverback. Gorillas make their homes by building something called a nest. While the number of mountain gorillas in the world is staying the same now, their numbers were declining in past years. There are very few left in the world.

1. a home made from parts of trees or plants: _____
2. the biggest or strongest male gorilla: _____
3. going down; getting lower: _____
4. people: _____
5. an animal which is like a large monkey with no tail: _____

The name 'Bwindi' means 'place of darkness.' The forests of the Bwindi Impenetrable National Park, Uganda, are certainly big and dark. This is especially true for a group of tourists very early in the morning. They're getting ready to start a long day of gorilla watching. The group hopes to have a chance to see gorillas in their natural forest environment.

As the tourists start their slow walk into the thick forest, they learn quickly that this is not going to be easy. Medad is their guide; his job is to show them where the gorillas are. As they walk, he explains where they're going to find the gorillas. He says: "These animals are called mountain gorillas, and mostly you find them on tops of mountains. So on our way, we should expect to be going up and down, up and down … " The group soon finds out that this is certainly true!

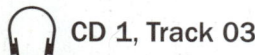 CD 1, Track 03

The tourists continue walking. They realize that they will probably have to walk a long way to see the gorillas. Then, suddenly, Medad gets a report. It's about the thirteen members of the group of gorillas called the 'M' group! They were seen at the far side of the forest. That means that they are many kilometers away.

"Here we go," says one of the tourists, and the group starts walking towards the 'M' group. They continue walking for a few hours. Finally, they reach a big hill that is covered in **mud**.[1] It's a very difficult walk, but the group makes it up the hill. They continue walking and looking, but they still don't see any gorillas.

---

[1]**mud:** a soft combination of water and earth

B7

Behavioral ecologist Michele Goldsmith has come along on the tour. Goldsmith's job is studying how gorillas act in their natural environment. She's been studying Bwindi's gorillas for five years.

Goldsmith knows where to find gorillas. She says that where they stay often depends on their food: "If they're in a place with very **dense vegetation**[2] that they're eating, they won't go very far. Sometimes they'll travel 300 [to] 400 **meters**[3] in a day. And then if there's maybe a preferred site they want to visit, they'll travel more than a kilometer."

---

[2]**dense vegetation:** a lot of plants
[3]**meter:** 1 meter = 3.3 feet; 1000 meters = 1 kilometer

The group keeps looking for the gorillas. There are more than 300 gorillas living in Bwindi Impenetrable National Park, but it's possible that the group won't see any of them. After some time, however, the tourists find gorilla nests, and gorilla **droppings**.[4] These are encouraging signs—the gorillas can't be far away!

The group continues walking, but stops very quickly. They've suddenly realized something. They are not 'watching' anything—something's watching them!

---

[4]**droppings:** waste produced by animals and birds

Predict

Answer the questions. Then scan page B12 to check your answers.

1. Who is watching the tourists?
2. What will the tourists do?

A young gorilla slowly stands up to look at the tourists. The tourists then realize that there are several gorillas in the area. They have found the group!

It starts raining, and the gorillas walk away to find **shelter**[5] from the rain under some big trees. The tourists follow carefully and try to get close to the gorilla family. The silverback—the big male gorilla—rests alone. Nearby, the tourists can see a mother with two young gorillas. The group is entertained by the young gorillas as they play in the trees. The tourists sit down for a while to watch them. This is exactly what they were hoping to see!

---

[5]**shelter:** protection from the weather

The gorillas go under the trees to find shelter from the rain.

When the rain stops, the gorillas start to move again. First the silverback leaves. Then, a mother goes with her baby on her back. Several small gorillas follow the larger and older gorillas. The younger ones have lots of energy! They run and play around the other gorillas as they move through the forest.

Since 1993 small groups of people have visited these apes almost every day. It's easy to see that these gorillas are used to human beings; they're relaxed when people are around them. This sense of comfort with people allows the tourists time to watch the gorillas. They can closely observe these beautiful animals in their own environment. But what do the gorillas do all day?

The gorillas spend most of their time eating. They eat leaves, **bark**,[6] fruit, and other plants. While the older gorillas eat, the younger gorillas play in the trees.

Finally, the silverback goes into the forest again. It's time for the tourists to leave. It's also time to end a very interesting day. This group of tourists was very fortunate. They were actually able to see gorillas in nature.

---

[6]**bark:** the hard outer covering of a tree

Scan for Information

Scan pages B14 and B16 to find the information.

1. In which year did people first come to visit the Bwindi gorillas?

2. What do gorillas spend most of their time doing?

3. What are four things gorillas eat?

The mountain gorillas of the Bwindi Impenetrable National Park are beautiful animals. Unfortunately, there are only about 700 mountain gorillas left in the world. The money from gorilla watching tours like this one may help conservation efforts. Will it be enough? No one knows.

In fact, there are many questions about the future of the mountain gorilla. Will the world find better methods of protecting them? Will their numbers increase or decline? Will the money from gorilla watching tours really help save them? Or will the beautiful gorillas of Bwindi **disappear**[7] from these forests forever?

---

[7]**disappear:** go away; leave suddenly

After You Read

1. What are the tourists thinking when they start their tour?
   A. The park feels big and dark.
   B. The gorillas are dangerous.
   C. It's late and cold.
   D. The gorillas are near.

2. In paragraph 1 on page B4, the word 'chance' means:
   A. look
   B. experience
   C. opportunity
   D. time

3. In paragraph 1 on page B7, the word 'they were seen' refers to the:
   A. tourists
   B. trees
   C. guides
   D. gorillas

4. According to Michele Goldsmith, which is true about the gorillas?
   A. They will not travel for food.
   B. They stay near food.
   C. They don't like the dense vegetation in the forest.
   D. They will travel more than a kilometer to find food.

5. Which is NOT a good heading for page B10?
   A. Good Signs, Getting Closer
   B. Apes See Tourists First
   C. Large Park, Long Walk
   D. No Gorillas to Watch Yet

6. The tourists finally found _____ gorillas.
   A. some
   B. any
   C. no
   D. most

7. Which kind of gorilla do the tourists NOT see?
   A. a mother
   B. a young gorilla
   C. a grandfather
   D. a silverback

8. In paragraph 2 on page B12, what does the word 'carefully' mean?
   A. quickly
   B. quietly
   C. closely
   D. suddenly

9. The gorillas probably feel that human beings are:
   A. happy
   B. dangerous
   C. unusual
   D. safe

10. It is important that gorillas have a sense of comfort with people because:
   A. The gorillas must eat often.
   B. Gorillas are beautiful.
   C. People come to see them often.
   D. People are not very careful.

11. Why were the tourists fortunate to visit the gorillas?
   A. because gorillas don't like people
   B. because there are so few gorillas
   C. because the gorillas don't like rain
   D. because the park isn't big enough

12. What is the main purpose of this story?
   A. to show a beautiful animal that needs help
   B. to discuss tourism in Uganda
   C. to teach about the silverback
   D. to introduce a Ugandan national park

The History of the National Park System

Today, there are thousands of national parks all over the world. The world's first national park was started in 1864. In that year, the United States government gave a large piece of land to the state of California. They asked the state to create a special park to protect the mountains and forests in the area. The trees in this area are called sequoias. The biggest ones are over one hundred meters high. They are the tallest living things in the world and are not found anywhere else on Earth.

Some sequoia trees are over one hundred meters high.

Conservationists in other countries saw what happened in California and soon began to do the same. Today Europe has over 350 national parks. The first one in France, Vanoise National Park, was created in 1963 because the government wanted to stop a plan to build a large tourist project there. The idea of creating a national park was first discussed in the 1940s, but people couldn't agree on what size to make the park. They also had different ideas on whether to put human or animal needs first. Ecologists worked with the government to finally agree on a plan that protected the animals, while still allowing some tourism.

The first national park in Germany opened in 1970. Like the first California park, the Bavarian Forest National Park was created to protect mountains and trees. It is the largest area of protected forest in Europe. The park has shelters where visitors can spend a night close to nature. In some places high up in the mountains, there are steps cut into the rock. This makes it easier for tourists to get to the top. Thousands of tourists go to the park each year. They walk through the attractive woods and enjoy the wonderful mountain views.

CD 1, Track 04

Word Count: 302
Time: _____

Vocabulary List

ape (B: 3, 14)
bark (B: 16)
conservation (B: 2, 18)
decline (B: 3, 18)
dense vegetation (B: 8)
disappear (B: 18)
droppings (B: 10)
ecologist (B: 2, 8)
forest (B: 2, 4, 7, 14, 16, 18)
gorilla (B: 2, 3, 4, 7, 8, 10, 12, 13, 14, 16, 17, 18)
guide (B: 2, 4)
human being (B: 3, 14)
meter (B: 8)
mud (B: 7)
national park (B: 2, 4, 10, 18)
nest (B: 3, 10)
shelter (B: 12, 13)
silverback (B: 3, 12, 14, 16)
tourist (B: 2, 4, 7, 10, 12, 14, 16)

Puffin Rescue!

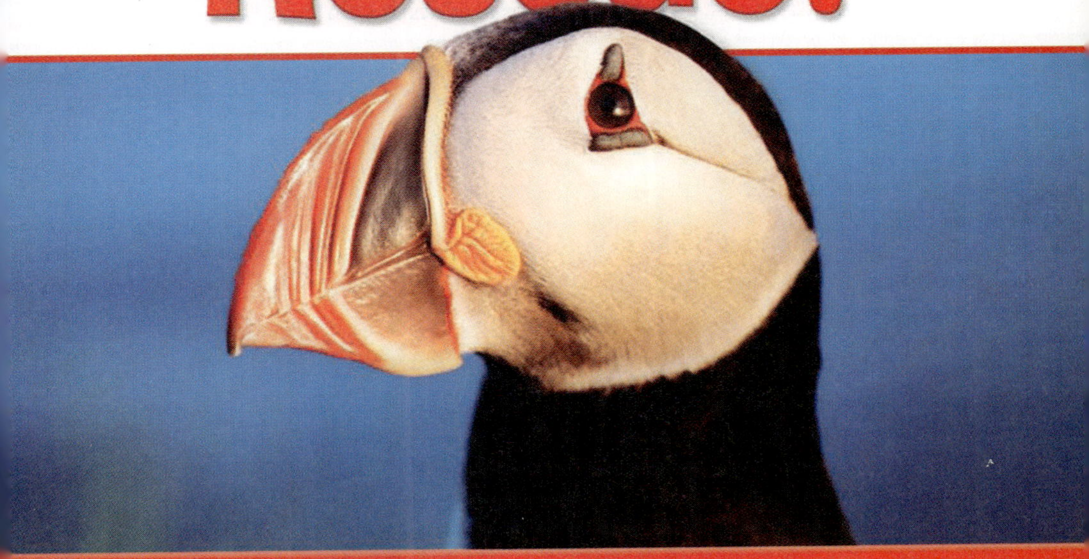

Rob Waring, *Series Editor*

HEINLE
CENGAGE Learning™

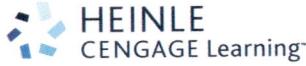

Australia • Brazil • Japan • Korea • Mexico • Singapore • Spain • United Kingdom • United States

Words to Know

This story is set in Iceland. Iceland is a country in Europe. The story happens in a small town called Heimaey [heɪmaɪ]. The town is on the south coast of Iceland.

A. Puffins.
Read the paragraph. Then complete the sentences with the underlined words.

This story is about puffins. Puffins are a kind of bird. The largest groups of puffins live in Iceland. Very young puffins are called pufflings. As they grow older, the pufflings try to fly away. However, sometimes, the pufflings become confused. They get lost and can't find the sea. Groups of people help these pufflings. These groups are called 'puffling patrols.' They rescue the pufflings and help them find the water.

1. _____ are a kind of bird that lives in Iceland.
2. _____ are young puffins.
3. _____ are groups of people that help puffins.
4. _____ means to save or keep safe.
5. A person or animal that does not understand something is _____.

A Puffling — A Puffin

B **A Seaside Town.** The town of Heimaey is by the sea. Here are some things you can find in a seaside town. Label the picture with the correct words.

| beach | cliff | dock | pier | sea |

1. _____
2. _____
3. _____
4. _____
5. _____

Einar and his sister Andrea are going to the beach to do a very important job. They have a box with them. Inside their box they have two helpless **orphans**[1] that they found on the streets of Heimaey, Iceland. What are they? They're young puffins!

Einar and Andrea hope to help the birds. They want to give them a **second chance**[2] at life. Einar explains why they want to do it. "They don't **survive**[3] if they stay in the town," he says. "Cats and dogs eat them, or they just die. It's really good to save them," he adds.

---

[1] **orphan:** a person or animal that has no mother or father
[2] **second chance:** another try
[3] **survive:** stay alive

 CD 1, Track 05

The children of Heimaey have been saving young puffins, or pufflings, for a long time. At the end of every summer, they help the lost pufflings find their way to the sea. It has become a tradition in the area around Heimaey.

Even the parents support the children and what they do. One parent reports, "They have to save the birds. If they don't do it, they die." She then adds that the children enjoy their work. "They find it very **exciting**,"[4] she says.

---

[4]**exciting:** fun and interesting

Predict

Answer the questions. Then scan page C8 to check your answers.

1. Why do the pufflings get lost?
2. What do the children do with lost pufflings?

While it is very exciting for the children, it may not always be enjoyable for the pufflings. However, it does save the young birds from danger. The children take the lost pufflings to the beach. Then they throw the pufflings into the air and watch them fly away. But why do the pufflings get lost in the first place?

When the young puffins are old enough, they leave their homes in the cliffs. They try to fly out to sea. But sometimes the lights from the town of Heimaey confuse them. This causes problems for pufflings. When this happens, the young puffins don't fly out to sea; they fly into the town!

Once they're in the town, the confused birds **crash into**[5] things. The people there find them on the streets of the city. That's when the children of Heimaey come to help. That's when they start having puffling patrols!

---

[5]**crash into:** run into; hit

Sequence the Events

What is the correct order of the events? Write numbers.

_____ The pufflings get lost.

_____ The pufflings leave the cliffs.

_____ The children find the pufflings.

_____ The children release the pufflings.

Each night at the end of the summer, moms and dads lead groups of children through town. They look for these lost pufflings. They use **flashlights**[6] to search the ground near buildings and street lights.

The pier is usually a good place to look for pufflings. When the children see a bird, they run to pick it up. They rescue the pufflings so they don't have to stay on the streets for the night. It's hard work, but it's fun, too.

---

[6]**flashlight:** a small light people can carry

puffling patrol

flashlight

A puffling patrol is looking for a lost puffling. Where is it?

At midnight, Olaf Holm and his six-year-old son Andrew are looking for pufflings. They look carefully around the docks. A half an hour later, they have a bird!

Olaf tells his story, "We came across the **parking lot**[7] and saw the **silhouette**.[8] [It] looked like a little puffin and sure enough—there he was! Right in the middle of the parking lot. We jumped out and we got him!"

---

[7]**parking lot:** a place where people keep their cars
[8]**silhouette:** shape or outline (of a puffin)

The next day, the puffling patrols take the rescued birds to the seashore. The children point the birds towards the ocean and release them. The children have a great time, but they must learn how to release the pufflings safely.

First, they must hold the puffin correctly. Next, they have to use the right style to throw the bird. It's almost like throwing a ball. Finally, they release the young puffin towards the sea! After that, it's up to the little puffin to swim or fly to safety.

Whether they swim or fly away, no one knows how this man-made problem really affects the puffins. There are eight to ten million puffins in Iceland. That's more than anywhere else in the world!

Fortunately, the yearly **search-and-rescue**[9] in Heimaey has become a big tradition. There, even lost pufflings get a second chance—all because of the strong arms and big hearts of the children of Heimaey!

---

[9]**search-and-rescue:** a plan to look for and save (puffins)

After You Read

1. What are Einar and his sister going to do at the beach?
   A. help some people
   B. clean the beach
   C. help some small birds
   D. play with puffins

2. According to page C4, why don't pufflings survive in Heimaey?
   A. People hurt them.
   B. Cars kill them.
   C. It's too cold.
   D. Animals eat them.

3. In paragraph 1 on page C7, 'they' refers to:
   A. pufflings
   B. orphans
   C. children
   D. cats

4. If the lost pufflings don't get help, _____ will die.
   A. it
   B. those
   C. they
   D. them

5. Where is the pufflings' home?
   A. the streets
   B. the cliffs
   C. the beach
   D. the docks

6. What's a good heading for page C8?
   A. Saving Lost Pufflings
   B. Birds Fly Home
   C. Town Lights
   D. Out to Sea

7. The puffling patrol does each of these EXCEPT:
   A. search near buildings
   B. check the beach
   C. go out at night
   D. take flashlights

8. On page C12, the word 'hard' in the phrase 'hard work' means:
   A. difficult
   B. boring
   C. dangerous
   D. terrible

9. In what direction should the puffins fly to safety?
   A. toward the town
   B. near the beach
   C. out to sea
   D. toward the lights

10. Why is rescuing puffins so popular in Iceland?
    A. Iceland's national bird is the puffin.
    B. People in Iceland love birds.
    C. Search-and-rescue is a hobby there.
    D. Iceland has a lot of puffins.

11. A person with a 'big heart' is each of these EXCEPT:
    A. kind
    B. confused
    C. friendly
    D. nice

12. The purpose of the last paragraph is to show that:
    A. Children have strong arms in Heimaey.
    B. Many puffins won't get a second chance.
    C. Children can make a difference in the world.
    D. The lost pufflings are safe in Iceland.

HEINLE Times

WHALE CAUGHT IN THAMES

As Martin Hewes looked out a train window in the middle of London, he thought he saw a whale in the River Thames. "That can't be!" he said to himself. While this kind of occurrence is not common, Hewes was wrong. Somehow, a northern bottlenose whale was caught in the River Thames. Whales don't usually appear in the middle of London. It's over twenty miles from the sea. The whale was about 20 feet long and weighed nearly 10,000 pounds. The appearance of the whale was exciting for the thousands of people who came to see it and to observe the rescue attempts.

A northern bottlenose whale was found in the River Thames.

Rescuers place the whale on a ship to try to save it.

No one is quite sure how the whale got into the difficult situation. Whales usually travel in groups and don't normally come near land. Scientists assume that this one lost contact with its group and became confused. The whale got into trouble when it entered the River Thames. The water wasn't deep enough for it to move easily. A whale is used to being in 2000 feet of water, and this water was less than 15 feet deep. The rocks at the base of the river cut into the whale. The rescue team said that as the whale tried to move around, it crashed into the sides of the river.

The next day, the rescue team attempted to lead the whale out toward the sea, but it was unable to move by itself. Its only chance for survival was to be put on a ship and carried out to sea. As the hours passed, the situation became even more serious. Unfortunately, in the end, the whale died. Many animal rescues are successful, but experiences like this one show us that no matter how hard we try, humans can't always change the course of nature.

CD 1, Track 06

Word Count: 319
Time: _____

Vocabulary List

beach (C: 3, 4, 8)
cliff (C: 3, 8, 11)
confuse (C: 2, 8, 10)
crash into (C: 10)
dock (C: 3, 14)
exciting (C: 7, 8)
flashlight (C: 13)
orphan (C: 4)
parking lot (C: 14)
pier (C: 3, 12)
puffin (C: 2, 4, 7, 8, 14, 16, 18)
puffling patrol (C: 2, 10, 12, 13, 16)
puffling (C: 2, 7, 8, 10, 11, 12, 13, 14, 16, 18)
rescue (C: 2, 12, 16, 18)
sea (C: 3, 8, 16)
search-and-rescue (C: 18)
second chance (C: 4)
silhouette (C: 14)
survive (C: 4)

A Disappearing WORLD

Rob Waring, *Series Editor*

Australia • Brazil • Japan • Korea • Mexico • Singapore • Spain • United Kingdom • United States

Words to Know

This story is set in Africa. It happens in the countries of Congo [kɒŋgoʊ] and Gabon [gæboʊn], in an area called the Congo Basin.

 An Expedition. Read the paragraph. Then match each word with the correct definition.

This story is about an expedition that travels through parts of Congo and Gabon. The trip starts just north of the equator. The leader of the trip, Michael Fay, is with the Wildlife Conservation Society. His team's aim is to document the wildlife of this beautiful and completely natural part of the world. They must do it before this natural beauty disappears and is gone forever. The biggest challenge for the group will be to cross the varied, and sometimes dangerous, landscape of the Congo Basin.

1. expedition _____
2. the equator _____
3. conservation _____
4. wildlife _____
5. disappear _____
6. challenge _____
7. landscape _____

a. animals and plants that live in natural conditions
b. an imaginary line around Earth's middle
c. a difficult task that tests one's skill or will
d. the features of a land area
e. the protection of plants, animals, or natural areas
f. a journey organized for a special purpose
g. go away suddenly and not return

B Wildlife in a Wild Land.
Here are some land formations on the expedition. Write the correct word next to each formation.

| hills | ocean | rain forest | rapids |

1. _____

2. _____

3. _____

4. _____

An Expedition

Distances
1 kilometer = .62 miles
1 meter = 3.3 feet

It's September in the Congo. Here, just north of the equator, an expedition unlike any other is about to begin. A team of scientists and researchers will travel for almost 2,000 kilometers through a rain forest in the middle of Africa. However, this isn't just any rain forest. This one covers over 150,000 **square kilometers**![1]

There has never been an expedition quite like this before. The aim of the expedition is to make a scientific record of the unusual and special world of the Congo Basin; a world which could be disappearing from Earth.

---

[1] **square kilometer:** the area of a square with sides of one kilometer

 CD 1, Track 07

Dr. Michael Fay is a scientist from the Wildlife Conservation Society. He is leading the group. He calls the expedition 'The Megatransect,' or 'the big crossing.' The expedition will go all the way across the Congo Basin. He and his team will travel around 2,000 kilometers through the rain forests of Congo and Gabon.

The conservation of this rain forest is very important to Fay. He feels the area is a very special place that's disappearing. He says that if they don't document the wildlife here now, there may never be another chance to do it. Fay explains in his own words: "What I'm trying to do, in a **desperate**[2] way, is to show the world that we're just about to lose the last little **gem**[3] in the African **continent**.[4] And if we don't do something now … if we don't do it today, we can forget about it."

---

[2]**desperate:** having an immediate, very strong need
[3]**gem:** a jewel; a very valuable thing
[4]**continent:** one of the main land areas of Earth

Infer Meaning

1. Why does Michael Fay feel 'desperate'?

2. What does Fay mean when he says "we can forget about it"?

The Congo Basin is one of the world's most important natural areas. It contains almost one quarter of the world's rain forests. It may also have up to half of all of the wild plants and animals found in all of Africa.

Fay's plan is to collect and record data on almost every part of the rain forest. He plans to do this by walking all the way through the forest. During this time, he wants to document the trees, the plants, and the animals that he sees there. It's a big job, and it's going to take a very long time.

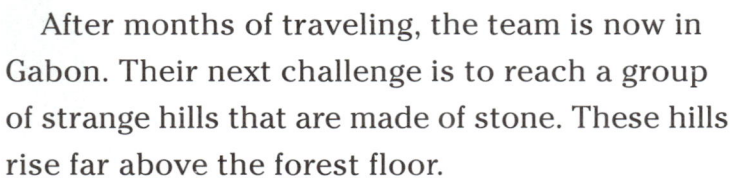

After months of traveling, the team is now in Gabon. Their next challenge is to reach a group of strange hills that are made of stone. These hills rise far above the forest floor.

The men reach the base of the hills. They slowly begin to walk up. Then, suddenly, they realize that they are finally above the tops of the trees. They have a wonderful view of everything around them!

From the top of the hills, the team can see very far in every direction.

Fay describes what the team can see. "We can see a long way here, you know … 70 or 80 kilometers in every direction. We can see **360 degrees**[5] around."

In today's world, it's unusual to be in a place where there are no other people. Fay also points this out. "There are no humans," he says. "There's not a single **village**,[6] there's not a single road." This makes it clear just how special and completely natural this African rain forest really is. "It's an **amazing**[7] place," he adds.

---

[5]**360 degrees:** a complete circle
[6]**village:** a group of houses that is a lot smaller than a town
[7]**amazing:** surprising; wonderful

The team continues on their long trip. As they go, they can hear their next challenge before they reach it. Rapids!

"Okay, wow," says Fay when he sees them—The **Kongou Chutes**.[8] These rapids are an important part of the landscape that the team wants to protect. This area is a land of fast-moving water and very old forests. Both of these things are currently in danger because of **logging**.[9] Businesses want to come here. They plan to cut down the trees so they can sell them as wood. If this happens, it will be very bad for the animals and plants in the area. It will also be bad for the land itself.

But, right now, the team has a more immediate problem. These rapids are very fast and very dangerous! According to Fay's plan, the team must cross the river here. Will they be able to cross safely? If they do, how will they do it?

---

[8] **Kongou Chutes:** [kɒŋgu ʃuts]
[9] **logging:** the work or industry of cutting trees

Predict

Answer the questions. Then scan page D16 to check your answers.

1. How will the team cross the dangerous rapids?

2. What will they need to do it?

The crossing is only a few hundred meters wide, but getting across it is not an easy task. The team members have a lot of experience. They use **guide ropes**,[10] **stepping stones**,[11] and everything they know to get across the dangerous waters safely.

After a lot of hard work, everyone finally makes it across the rapids. However, the team has to spend a lot of time doing it. It takes them a full day to get themselves and their supplies across the rapids, and they still have a very long way to go!

---

[10]**guide rope:** a thick cord that people follow to find a way
[11]**stepping stone:** small stones, usually in water, that people walk on

stepping stones

After more than a year, the team finally reaches the end of their travels. They are at the Atlantic Ocean at last, and they are all very pleased to be there. Later, Fay describes how he felt as he took those final steps through the rain forest. "We'd been walking in the woods in our own little world for fifteen months and now it was over," he says. "I was **overwhelmed**."[12]

In the end, Dr. Michael Fay and his team walked around 2,000 kilometers through some of the wildest lands of Africa. Along the way, they documented as many of the things they found as possible. They did it all as part of the challenging scientific expedition called 'The Megatransect.' They also did it in an attempt to save a disappearing world.

---

[12] **overwhelmed:** having a very strong feeling

After You Read

1. Compared to other rain forests, the Congo Basin is:
   A. small
   B. average size
   C. dark
   D. large

2. What is the main purpose of the expedition?
   A. to study and record information
   B. to walk a long way
   C. to disappear
   D. to meet people

3. In paragraph 2 on page D6, the word 'we' refers to:
   A. the Wildlife Conservation Society
   B. the people of the world
   C. scientists
   D. the Megatransect

4. Dr. Michael Fay thinks the Congo Basin is:
   A. safe
   B. fortunate
   C. in trouble
   D. forgettable

5. In paragraph 1 on page D8, the word 'contains' can be replaced by:
   A. collects
   B. has
   C. records
   D. takes

6. The Congo Basin has _____ of the plants found in Africa.
   A. all
   B. a few
   C. none
   D. many

7. Which will Dr. Fay probably NOT document during his trip?
   A. trees
   B. people
   C. animals
   D. plants

8. Which is a good heading for page D10?
   A. A View of Everything
   B. No Animals, No Village
   C. Team Can See a Short Way
   D. Low Stone Hills

9. In paragraph 1 on page D13, the word 'describes' can be replaced by:
   A. asks
   B. tells about
   C. wonders
   D. believes

10. Who is 'they' in the phrase 'they plan to cut' on page D14?
    A. the expedition
    B. the animals
    C. logging businesses
    D. the Kongou Chutes

11. What does the team use to cross the rapids?
    A. stepping stones
    B. guide ropes
    C. experience
    D. all of the above

12. Crossing the Kongou Chutes is a _____ task.
    A. slow
    B. simple
    C. quick
    D. safe

The Wildlife Conservation Society
WHAT IS IT?

The goal of the Wildlife Conservation Society (WCS) is to protect a wide range of animals. Some of the world's animals are endangered, or currently in danger of disappearing from the earth. The WCS is also involved in the protection of animal environments. Saving these natural areas of land will allow certain animals to live and increase in number. The challenge of this work is becoming increasingly difficult. Humans are taking over more of the places where animals used to live.

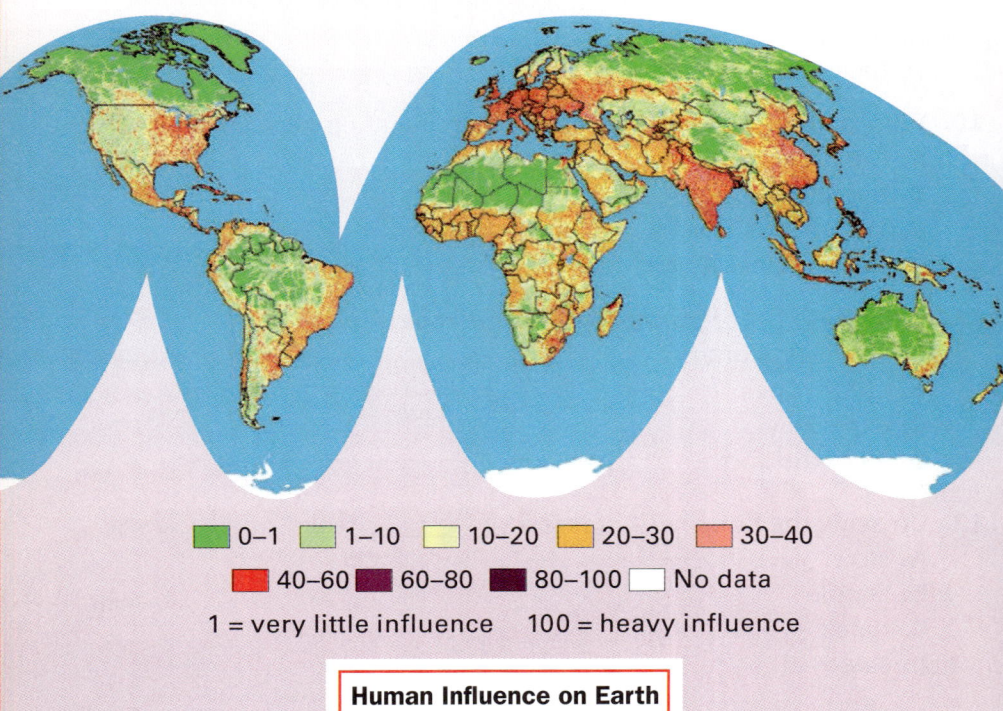

0–1   1–10   10–20   20–30   30–40
40–60   60–80   80–100   No data
1 = very little influence   100 = heavy influence

Human Influence on Earth

Source: World Wildlife Fund/U.S. Conservation Science Program

The WCS works in four major areas:

SCIENCE

Over a hundred years ago, the WCS added its first animal specialist, Dr. Reid Blair, to its staff. Since then, the WCS Wildlife Health Sciences Division has become a world leader in this field. Today, these study and research activities help care for more than 17,000 animals in parks in the United States and around the world.

INTERNATIONAL CONSERVATION

Humans now live on most parts of the earth. People must carefully consider how to best use the few untouched areas that remain. They must also give special consideration to endangered animals. The WCS land conservation program concentrates on these areas.

EDUCATION

The 'Living Landscapes' program is just one way the WCS helps to protect endangered animals. It provides parks where endangered animals can live safely, which is an important first step. However, animals don't know

> "Humans are taking over more of the places where animals used to live."

where these parks end. Therefore, local people must also learn how to treat the animals outside of the park area. The Living Landscapes Program helps to educate local communities.

CITY WILDLIFE PARKS

Since 1895, the main WCS office has been in the largest park in New York. School children visit city parks every day of the week to learn about conservation. Several programs are available in the park system, including family events, discovery centers where people can experience the wildlife, and wildlife theaters.

CD 1, Track 08

Word Count: 315
Time: _____

Vocabulary List

360 degrees (D: 13)
amazing (D: 13)
challenge (D: 2, 10, 14, 19)
conservation (D: 2, 6)
continent (D: 6)
desperate (D: 6, 7, 19)
disappear (D: 2, 4, 6, 19)
equator (D: 2, 4)
expedition (D: 2, 3, 4, 6, 19)
gem (D: 6)
guide rope (D: 16, 17)
hill (D: 3, 10, 11)
landscape (D: 2, 14)
logging (D: 14)
ocean (D: 3, 19)
overwhelm (D: 19)
rain forest (D: 3, 4, 6, 8, 10, 13, 19)
rapids (D: 3, 14, 15, 16)
square kilometer (D: 4)
stepping stones (D: 16)
village (D: 13)
wildlife (D: 2, 3, 6, 19)

The Knife Markets OF SANAA

Rob Waring, *Series Editor*

Australia • Brazil • Japan • Korea • Mexico • Singapore • Spain • United Kingdom • United States

Words to Know

This story is set in a country in the Middle East called Yemen [yɛmən]. It happens in the city of Sanaa [sɑnɑ].

A In the *Souq*.
Read the paragraph. Use the correct form of the underlined words to complete the definitions.

There are *souqs* [suks], or <u>markets</u>, in many countries in the Middle East. *Souqs* are full of small <u>stalls</u> where people can buy <u>spices</u> for food, beautiful <u>jewelry</u>, and special <u>knives</u>. These knives are often heavily <u>decorated</u> and are very expensive. However, the high cost is not only related to money.

1. A place where people go to buy and sell things is a _____.

2. _____ are tools used for cutting.

3. Objects that people wear to look more attractive are _____.

4. _____ are plant-based products that add flavor to food.

5. A small shop with an open front in a public place is a _____.

6. _____ means that something has been added to an item to make it more attractive.

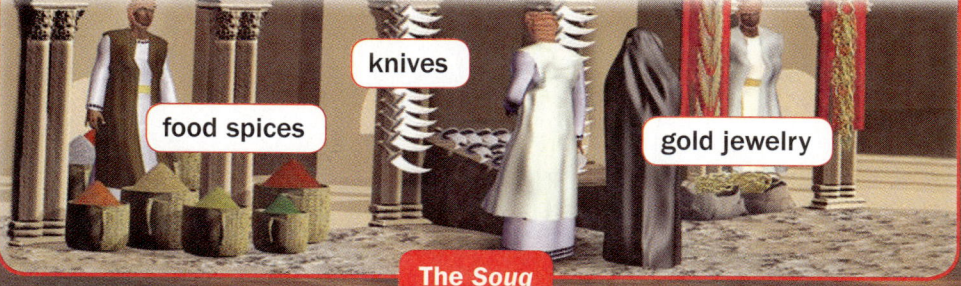

The *Souq*

B. The *Jambiya*. Read the paragraph, then look at the pictures. Write the correct item number next to each **bolded** word.

The *jambiya* [dʒæmbiə] is very important to the men of Yemen. This special knife has a hooked, or rounded, **blade** ( ). The men of Yemen usually wear a *jambiya* in their **belt** ( ). The **handle** ( ) of the *jambiya* is often made from a **rhinoceros' horn** ( ). It can also be made from **water buffalo horns** ( ), or **camel hooves** ( ).

A *Jambiya* in a Man's Belt

It is the beginning of the day in the ancient city of Sanaa, Yemen. The morning **call to prayer**[1] wakes the people who live in this beautiful city. This call to prayer has been the same for hundreds of years here.

Sanaa, Yemen's capital city, is in one of the higher areas of Yemen. It has many mountains and hills around it. It's a very special place in many ways. This beautiful city is one of the oldest cities in the world. People have lived here for thousands of years!

---

[1] **call to prayer:** a sound that tells Muslim people that it's time to show respect to their god

 CD 1, Track 09

In the more ancient parts of the city, there are several very tall houses. These houses are made from **mud**[2] and are very close together. They're also covered with white **plaster**.[3] To some, this combination makes Sanaa look like a city that is made of **gingerbread**.[4]

---

[2]**mud:** a soft combination of water and earth
[3]**plaster:** a white material that is put on walls of buildings
[4]**gingerbread:** a kind of cake that is decorated with white topping

Some people think that the mud and white plaster houses of Sanaa look like cake!

Sanaa is a place of beauty and tradition. Here, the busy *souqs* of the city are spread out over several streets. In these *souqs*, the people of Yemen, or Yemenis, **bargain**[5] for spices, jewelry, and other products. People have done this traditional activity for hundreds of years.

Throughout the day, people buy and sell a lot of different and interesting items at the stalls in these markets. However, there is one thing here that is very special to the people of Yemen. Any visitor who walks through the streets of the *souq* will quickly notice it: the *jambiya*.

---

[5]**bargain:** when a buyer and seller work together to agree on a price

The *jambiya* is something that most Yemeni men are hardly ever without. These large, beautifully decorated knives are very important here. Because they are so important, the men of Yemen usually wear the knives in a special thick belt. They want everyone to be able to see their *jambiya*. They want people to see how big, beautiful, or specially decorated their knives are.

The *jambiya*, with its large blade, may look dangerous to some people. However, these days it's almost never used as a **weapon**.[6] It is a **status symbol**[7] and a sign of Yemeni **manhood**.[8]

---

[6]**weapon:** object used in fighting or war, such as a gun or knife
[7]**status symbol:** something that shows that a person is important
[8]**manhood:** qualities related to being a man and not a boy

In the busy market, **blacksmiths**[9] carefully shape metal into the unusual hooked blades. These very special knives are everywhere in the *souq*. Several of the stalls have rows of the beautiful *jambiya* for people to look at and buy.

---

[9]**blacksmith:** someone whose job is to make things from metal

a row of *jambiya* knives

Blacksmiths shape metal into jambiya blades.

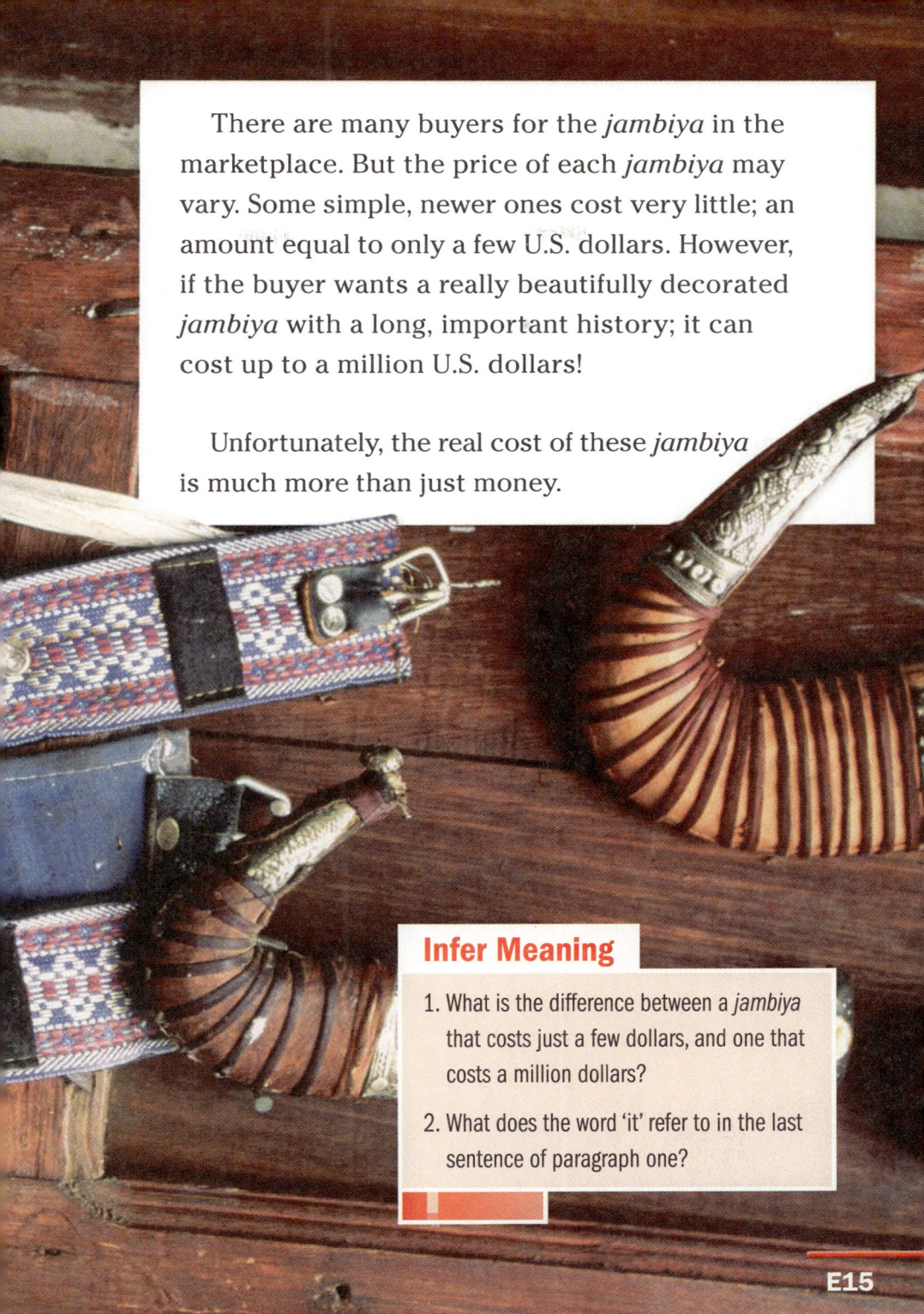

There are many buyers for the *jambiya* in the marketplace. But the price of each *jambiya* may vary. Some simple, newer ones cost very little; an amount equal to only a few U.S. dollars. However, if the buyer wants a really beautifully decorated *jambiya* with a long, important history; it can cost up to a million U.S. dollars!

Unfortunately, the real cost of these *jambiya* is much more than just money.

Infer Meaning

1. What is the difference between a *jambiya* that costs just a few dollars, and one that costs a million dollars?
2. What does the word 'it' refer to in the last sentence of paragraph one?

The value of these knives often depends on the handle, which is traditionally made from rhinoceros horn. Yemeni knife makers prefer to use rhinoceros horn because it makes the handle very attractive. Because rhinoceros horn is used on *jambiya* handles, many people think the *jambiya* is part of a big problem; the illegal killing of rhinos. These beautiful and unusual animals are in danger. Too many people are killing them to make *jambiya* handles and other things. Soon, there may be none left.

Now, the Yemeni government and international groups are working together. They're trying to stop people from buying and selling rhinoceros horns. However, the tradition of using rhinoceros horn on *jambiya* is very strong. Some knife makers will not stop using this material.

Conservationists[10] and government members are also trying another way to get the knife makers to change. They are encouraging them to use other materials for *jambiya* handles. They want the knife makers to use water buffalo horn or camel hooves for the handles instead. But in Yemen, tradition is very strong, and change is sometimes slow. Unfortunately, a *jambiya* that is made from rhinoceros horn may still be a status symbol here for a long time to come.

---

[10]**conservationist:** someone who works to save or protect the environment

What do you think?

1. How do you feel about using animals to make products for sale?
2. What other things can the Yemeni government do to stop knife makers from using rhinoceros horn?

After You Read

1. Which is NOT true about the morning call to prayer?
   A. It happens early.
   B. It happens only in ancient cities.
   C. It happens in Yemen.
   D. It has happened for a long time.

2. In paragraph 2 on page E4, 'it' in 'it has many' refers to:
   A. higher areas
   B. Yemen
   C. Yemen's capital city
   D. tall houses

3. Which is a good heading for page E6?
   A. People of Sanaa Like Gingerbread
   B. Living Inside a Cake House
   C. Mud and Plaster Make Gingerbread
   D. Homes Look Like Decorated Cake

4. Which do people buy in the markets?
   A. spices
   B. traditions
   C. *souqs*
   D. houses

5. In paragraph 2 on page E9, 'throughout' means:
   A. without
   B. in the middle of
   C. during
   D. especially in

6. The *jambiya* is a special traditional knife worn _____ Yemeni men.
   A. in
   B. by
   C. with
   D. of

7. For Yemeni men, what is the *jambiya* a symbol of?
  A. childhood
  B. fighting
  C. danger
  D. importance

8. *Jambiya* are _____ bought in the markets of Sanaa.
  A. rarely
  B. sometimes
  C. often
  D. never

9. In paragraph 1 on page E16, what does 'illegal' mean?
  A. not allowed
  B. traditional
  C. uncontrolled
  D. apparent

10. What is the main purpose of page E16?
  A. to explain why there is a problem with *jambiya*
  B. to show the beauty of the knives in detail
  C. to communicate that rhinos are not in danger
  D. to teach how the knives are so unusual

11. The Yemeni government wants the knives to be made from:
  A. rhinoceros horns
  B. water buffalo horns
  C. camel horns
  D. all of the above

12. What does the writer think will probably happen to the handles?
  A. They will be made from a new material soon.
  B. The knife makers will stop making them.
  C. The conservationists will make change happen.
  D. Nothing will change quickly.

Dear Sarah,

Thanks for your letter. How are you? I have lots of news for you! I have finally arrived in Savannakhet, Laos. I started my new job last week and I've had a lot to do ever since. Right now it's 6:00 in the morning and I've just returned from shopping in the morning market. I know 6:00 is really early, but the market actually opens at 5:00! If you arrive any later than 5:30, all the best food has been sold.

The morning market is really interesting. It's in an old building, however, the building doesn't have a floor. You actually walk through mud inside it! Most of the sellers sit in stalls with their products displayed on the ground in front of them. The market is divided into sections. The food is in one area, the jewelry in another, and clothing in another. Outside of the market, some men sell objects that they have made by hand. However, most of the sellers at the market are women. It's generally the women who make and sell the products.

Savannakhet is in the south of Laos.

Morning Market

    I don't have any way to keep food cold, so shopping has become an everyday activity for me. Bargaining is a big part of shopping in Laos. When I came here, I didn't know anything about this skill. It has not been easy for me to learn. I understood quickly that it's necessary to bargain for everything you buy. If you don't bargain, it's a bad message to people here. It's like saying, "I have lots of money. I don't need to talk about price with you." I enjoy bargaining now as it is a chance to communicate with local people. The morning market allows me to practice my Laotian language skills. They're improving all the time!

    I still want to tell you about the evening market, but that will have to wait for another letter!

    Your brother,
    John

CD 1, Track 10

Word Count: 320
Time: _____

Vocabulary List

bargain (E: 9)
belt (E: 3, 10, 13)
blacksmith (E: 12, 13)
blade (E: 3, 10, 12)
call to prayer (E: 4)
camel hooves (E: 3, 19)
conservationist (E: 19)
decorate (E: 2, 6, 10, 15)
gingerbread (E: 6)
handle (E: 3, 16, 19)
jewelry (E: 2, 9)
knife (E: 2, 3, 10, 12, 16, 19)
manhood (E: 10)
market (E: 2, 9, 15)
mud (E: 6, 7)
plaster (E: 6, 7)
rhinoceros horn (E: 3, 16, 19)
spice (E: 2, 9)
stall (E: 2, 9, 12)
status symbol (E: 10, 19)
water buffalo horn (E: 3, 19)
weapon (E: 10)

A Special Kind of Neighborhood

Rob Waring, *Series Editor*

Australia • Brazil • Japan • Korea • Mexico • Singapore • Spain • United Kingdom • United States

Words to Know

This story is set the United States (U.S.), in the state of California. It takes place in the city of San Francisco. [sæn frənsɪskoʊ]

 A Multicultural Neighborhood. Read the paragraph. Then complete the sentences with the correct form of the underlined words.

    This story is about an old neighborhood in San Francisco called the Mission District or 'The Mission' for short. This neighborhood started near a church called Mission Dolores. Spanish missionaries started the church in 1791. They wanted to teach people about their beliefs. Now, many people from other countries live in The Mission. The majority of these immigrants are Latino. They come from Central and South America. This has made the community that lives in the area very multicultural.

1. An area of a city is called a n_____.
2. People who travel around and teach about their god are m_____.
3. A place where people pray to a god is a c_____.
4. Something that is related to traditions and beliefs from many different countries is m_____.
5. A group of people who live in the same area form a c_____.
6. People who move to another country to live are i_____.
7. People from Central or South America are also known as L_____.

B **Things to Do in the Mission District.** Here are some different activities people do in the Mission District. Write the letter of each phrase next to the correct activity.

> **a.** sing in the choir
> **b.** paint murals
> **c.** play music
> **d.** eat Latin-American food

San Francisco's Mission Dolores was built in 1791.

Each Sunday, people can hear the music of the Mission Dolores Basilica in San Francisco. With the sound comes memories of the Spanish missionaries who built the church in 1791. They didn't know it at the time, but it was the start of a special kind of neighborhood: the Mission District.

The area is a place with a long and varied history. One member of the community describes it as a central part of San Francisco, because it's near where the city began long ago. He adds that it's important for people to understand the many levels of history in the neighborhood. He feels that this knowledge is a big part of understanding what it means to be a real San Franciscan.

 CD 2, Track 01

Fact Check: True or false?

1. The Mission District started in 1791.
2. Spanish missionaries built the church.
3. The Mission District has many layers of history.

One of the most interesting parts of the Mission District is its people. Over the years, immigrants have come to the area from Ireland, Germany, and Italy. But the most recent immigrants are mainly from Mexico and countries in Central and South America. It's easy to see the style that these recent additions give to the neighborhood. You can see it in the art on the walls, taste it in the food, and hear it in the music!

Juan Pedro Gaffney grew up in the Mission District. He's the director of the Spanish Choir of San Francisco. In the past, his group has performed to raise money for people after **natural disasters**[1] in Central America. Many people in the choir are very close to these countries. Juan Pedro explains that the people of the Mission District share the pain and the happiness of their friends and relatives in Latin America. He says that the local community feels a sense of common involvement. They really care when a neighboring nation is in pain.

---

[1] **natural disaster:** natural event that causes a lot of damage and serious problems

During good times or bad, the music of The Mission deeply affects everyone. Sometimes it helps people to share their sadness. Sometimes it helps them to enjoy life. Juan Pedro explains that music has always been a basic part of **cultural identity**[2] in The Mission. He feels that the music of the district is colorful and lively. And, according to him, it's absolutely "**jumping**"![3]

But it isn't just the music that's colorful and lively in the Mission District. The art of The Mission is full of life as well.

---

[2]**cultural identity:** sense of closeness to one's culture and environment
[3]**jumping:** (slang) very fun and energetic

The local art community of The Mission stays close to the area's culture and tradition. A local arts organization often leads people on walks through the district. They visit streets like Balmy Alley, which is famous for its murals.

Artist Ray Patlan talks about the art of the Mission District. "What happens is, the murals begin to reflect the community itself," he says. In 1984, Patlan helped to organize a group of artists to paint a series of murals here. The theme at the time was 'Peace in Central America.'

Nowadays however, while the district remains mainly Latino, it's no longer 1984. The political situation is no longer the same either. Patlan points out that both politics and the world have changed over the years. He then adds that because of this, the art of The Mission has changed as well. He explains that the art of the area is a part of the streets, and it's also a reflection of the community. So, as the community changes, people can see changes in the murals as well.

Even though the meanings behind the murals are always changing, they are still very powerful. Apparently, they're something the community likes, too. Andrea Coombes lives in The Mission. "It's great," she says. "It's like coming home to a piece of art every day. Every time we drive up it's just very **vibrant**!"[4]

---

[4]**vibrant:** lively and interesting

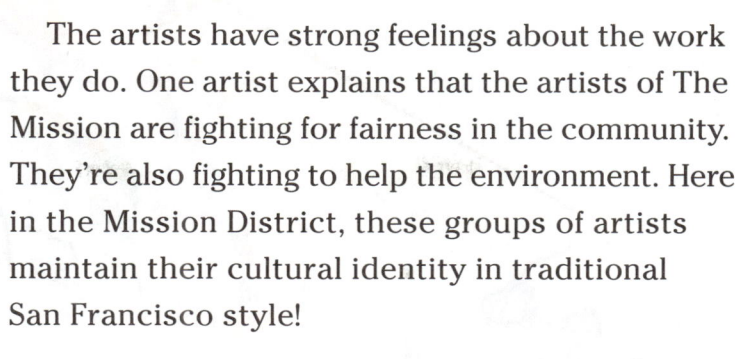

The artists have strong feelings about the work they do. One artist explains that the artists of The Mission are fighting for fairness in the community. They're also fighting to help the environment. Here in the Mission District, these groups of artists maintain their cultural identity in traditional San Francisco style!

Many of these artists feel that The Mission is a successful neighborhood where new immigrants are welcome. "People see that they're not so different from each other," says one artist. "There [are] a lot of things that **bind**[5] [the immigrants] through culture and tradition."

---

[5]**bind:** unite; bring together

The members of Saint Peter's Church are another group that understands the closeness between culture and tradition. Mission Dolores was the **foundation**[6] of the Mission District, but Saint Peter's is another strong base in the area.

Father Dan McGuire is the leader of Saint Peter's. He talks about all the different cultures that form the community around the church. "The beauty of this particular **parish**,"[7] says Father McGuire, "is that the different cultures from Latin America and the different countries of Latin America come together here. And they really form a common unity." The people who go to the church are from countries such as Mexico, El Salvador, and Peru. They come from all over Latin America!

---

[6]**foundation:** starting point; base
[7]**parish:** an area that has its own church

Immigrants from Latin America make up a big part of the community of the Mission District.

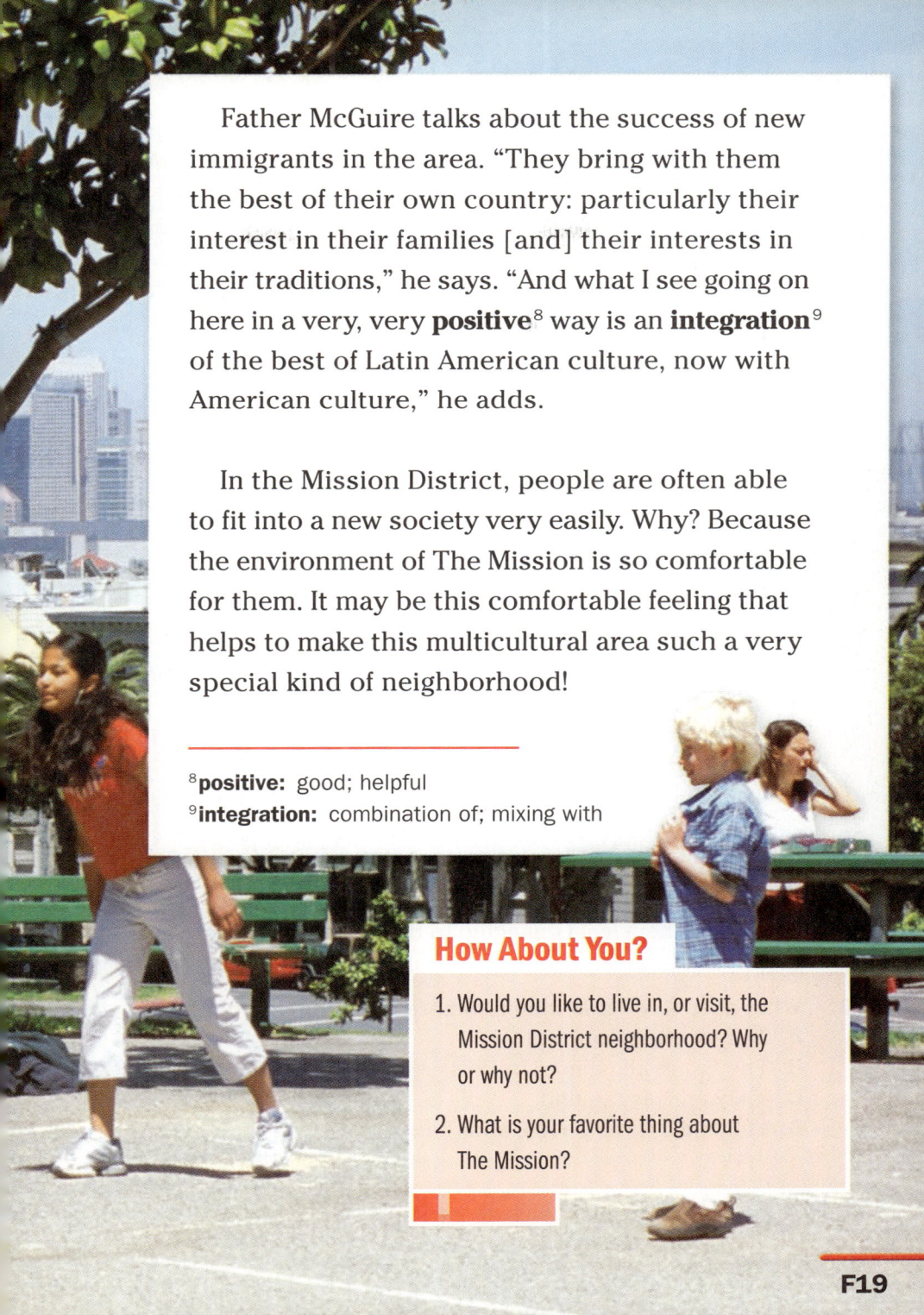

Father McGuire talks about the success of new immigrants in the area. "They bring with them the best of their own country: particularly their interest in their families [and] their interests in their traditions," he says. "And what I see going on here in a very, very **positive**[8] way is an **integration**[9] of the best of Latin American culture, now with American culture," he adds.

In the Mission District, people are often able to fit into a new society very easily. Why? Because the environment of The Mission is so comfortable for them. It may be this comfortable feeling that helps to make this multicultural area such a very special kind of neighborhood!

[8]**positive:** good; helpful
[9]**integration:** combination of; mixing with

How About You?

1. Would you like to live in, or visit, the Mission District neighborhood? Why or why not?
2. What is your favorite thing about The Mission?

After You Read

1. The Mission District is a _____.
   A. church
   B. community
   C. memory
   D. city

2. In paragraph 1 on page F5, the word 'they' refers to people:
   A. who were missionaries in 1791
   B. at church on Sunday
   C. in the neighborhood
   D. living in San Francisco

3. Which is NOT a good heading for page F7?
   A. What is The Mission?
   B. Helping Countries in Pain
   C. Not Enough Money Raised
   D. Interesting People from Many Places

4. In paragraph 1 on page F8, the word 'deeply' can be replaced by:
   A. greatly
   B. badly
   C. directly
   D. lively

5. How does the music of the Mission District affect people?
   A. It helps them when they're happy.
   B. It helps them when they're sad.
   C. It helps them feel connected to their environment.
   D. all of the above

6. What does Ray Patlan think is important about the murals?
   A. They are very colorful.
   B. They were all painted in 1984.
   C. They are easy to find.
   D. They reflect the people and times.

7. In paragraph 2 on page F12, the word 'they' refers to:
   A. the artists
   B. the murals
   C. the neighbors
   D. politicians

8. A good heading for page F15 is:
   A. Mission Artists Fight for Fairness and Change
   B. Industrial Artists Look for Cultural Identity
   C. Traditional San Francisco Style Missing in Mission
   D. People Cannot Connect Through Mural Art

9. The Mission is a lively and interesting neighborhood _____ many different people.
   A. where
   B. from
   C. in
   D. with

10. Father Dan McGuire believes that the people in The Mission:
   A. have formed a common community
   B. are from Europe
   C. must come to his parish
   D. come from Saint Peter's

11. In paragraph 1 on page F16, the word 'base' can be replaced by:
   A. parish
   B. house
   C. center
   D. church

12. Which word best describes the Mission District?
   A. successful
   B. vibrant
   C. united
   D. all of the above

A New Berlin

The old Berlin was known for its fine music, food, and art. Its streets were full of historical buildings and there were beautiful views everywhere. However, for 28 years, from 1961 to 1989, the city was divided into East and West Berlin by the Berlin Wall. This wall separated two areas that were controlled by different powers. During this time, Berlin lost some of its liveliness.

Nowadays, however, the city has many immigrant groups and a rising art and music culture. Berlin has become one of the most vibrant, multicultural cities in Europe. Today, about 3.5 million people live there. A half a million of these people were not born in Germany. These immigrants have come from 185 different countries. Many live in communities with other people from their homelands. Each of these neighborhoods is a great place to see and each has a very different look and feel.

Some Multicultural Neighborhoods of Berlin

Each year, thousands of people attend Berlin's art fairs.

Kreuzberg

Many people from the country of Turkey now live in the area of Kreuzberg. This is a lively, happy area. In addition to all the special foods from Turkey and the bookstores, you will also find nightclubs here. In these clubs, young people from many different cultures come together to play music and dance all night.

Art Mile

In the recent past, most artists lived and worked in West Berlin. But today everything has changed. The 'Art Mile' was an area in East Berlin that wasn't very interesting in the past. It is now the city's lively art center. Berlin has two international art events in the 'Art Mile.' These events attract thousands of visitors from around the world each year.

Prenzlauer Berg

Visitors love the neighborhood called Prenzlauer Berg. Its streets are jumping with the energy of all the musicians, artists, and designers who live and work there. But there are also quiet, restful shops where people drink tea, read books, or write their own stories.

CD 2, Track 02

Word Count: 326
Time: _____

Vocabulary List

bind (F: 15)
choir (F: 3, 7)
church (F: 2, 5, 16)
community (F: 2, 5, 7, 11, 12, 15, 16, 17)
cultural identity (F: 8, 15)
foundation (F: 16)
immigrant (F: 2, 7, 15, 17, 19)
integration (F: 19)
jumping (F: 8)
Latino (F: 2, 12)
missionaries (F: 2, 5)
multicultural (F: 2, 19)
mural (F: 3, 11, 12)
music (F: 3, 5, 7, 8)
natural disaster (F: 7)
neighborhood (F: 2, 5, 7, 15, 16, 19)
parish (F: 16)
positive (F: 19)
vibrant (F: 12)

The Last of the
CHEJU DIVERS

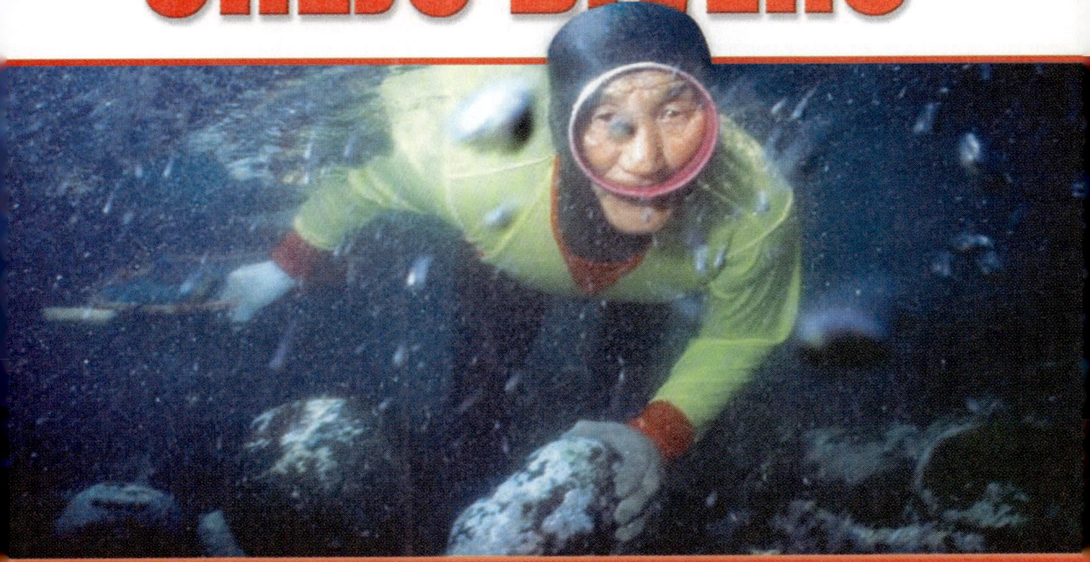

Rob Waring, *Series Editor*

Australia • Brazil • Japan • Korea • Mexico • Singapore • Spain • United Kingdom • United States

Words to Know

This story is set in South Korea. It happens in a place called Cheju [tʃeɪdʒu] Island.

A Scuba Divers.
Label the picture with the underlined words in the paragraph.

Divers are people who go underwater for enjoyment or their job. Scuba divers use an oxygen tank. It allows them to breathe underwater. Sometimes divers go into the ocean to find seafood. Octopus, abalone, and sea urchin are common seafoods.

3. _____

2. _____

1. _____

4. _____

octopus

sea urchin

abalone

B Cheju Divers.
Read the paragraph. Then match each word with the correct definition.

Cheju is a small island that is known for its legendary women divers. It's also a society that is changing. In the past, women in Cheju often had to become divers, or *Haenyos* [haɪnyoʊs], to get money. It was dangerous, but there was no other way to make a living. Recently, more tourists are coming to the island. The young women of Cheju now have more job choices. This story is about the differences between these two generations of women. It's about a young tour guide and her 63-year-old aunt, who is one of the last of the Cheju divers.

1. legendary _____
2. make a living _____
3. tourist _____
4. choice _____
5. generation _____
6. tour guide _____
7. aunt _____

a. a visitor who travels for enjoyment
b. people of a similar age within a society or family
c. the sister of someone's father or mother
d. possibility to pick one option out of many
e. famous; having been around for a long time
f. earn money for shelter, food, and other necessities
g. a person who shows visitors around and gives information about a place

A Cheju Diver

The island of Cheju off the coast of South Korea is known for its natural beauty. It's also known for its **volcanoes**,[1] which are no longer active. However, Cheju is also famous for something a little more unusual. It's famous for a group of legendary women divers called *haenyos*.

These women dive into the sea every day to look for seafood. It's their job, and it's difficult and very dangerous work. They make these dives without oxygen tanks. They can **hold their breath**[2] and stay underwater for up to five minutes!

---

[1] **volcano:** a mountain with a hole in the top
[2] **hold (ones) breath:** not take additional air into the body; keep air in the lungs

 CD 2, Track 03

For hundreds of years, the women of Cheju Island have made their living from deep within the sea. They dive into the cold waters and catch octopus, abalone, and sea urchins. The seafood they catch has fed the people of Cheju for a very long time. However, the present generation of women divers on Cheju may be the last one. Things on this small island are starting to change.

Sunny Hong is part of a new generation of Cheju women. She's a tour guide. Her life doesn't depend on catching seafood from the ocean. It depends on the tourists that have started visiting the island.

Sunny thinks that the job is just right for her. She says, "I wanted to find some kind of job [in] which I can use my English, and also this kind of job fit[s] my **aptitude**."[3]

---

[3]**aptitude:** *(unusual use)* natural ability or skill

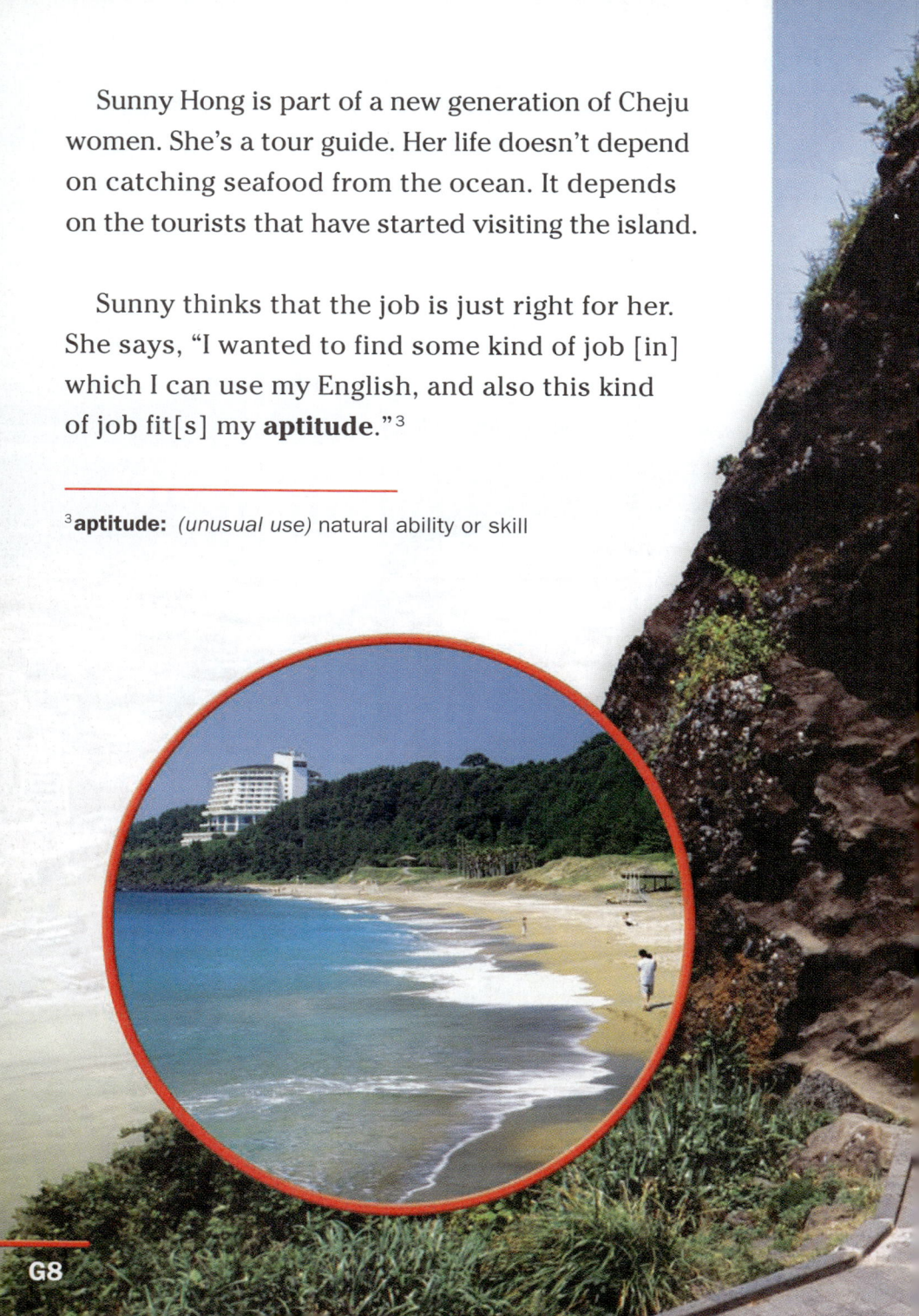

Sunny has taught herself English. It is this skill that has made her successful on land rather than having to depend on the sea. Until now, all of her female family members have worked in the ocean as divers.

Sunny introduces her aunt, Ho Hong. "This is my aunt, Ms. Hong. She's 63 years old and she started diving when she was thirteen," Sunny explains, "so [she has been diving for] almost fifty years now." Sunny's aunt and her diver friends have been diving nearly all of their lives!

How did these women get started in such an unusual and sometimes dangerous job? Sunny explains for her aunt: "They didn't have a choice. Also, they were born in [a] sea village, so they had to be a woman diver, and there [was] nothing they [could] do except [be a] woman diver."

It's clear why the women didn't always choose to be divers. The job is very dangerous. In fact, it's the most dangerous job on the island, and it's only done by women. But what makes it so dangerous?

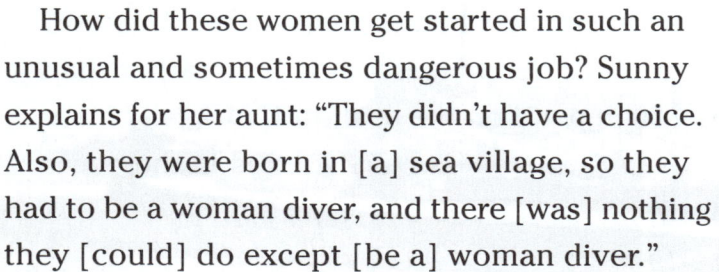

Predict

Answer the questions with 'True' or 'False'. Then, check your answers on page G15.

1. Divers often develop problems with their ears.

2. Divers never die underwater.

3. Divers can get serious pains in their bodies.

When they go down into the sea, the divers sometimes develop pains in their bodies. They can also experience very serious problems with their ears. Strong **tides and currents**[4] can even cause the divers to **drown**.[5] But the *haenyos* continue to dive, and they often do it for years.

This last generation of women divers is not a young one. The youngest diver on the island is 45 years old. The oldest diver is 75. These women dive for five to six hours every day! But, why do they keep diving for so long?

---

[4]**tides and currents:** movements of the ocean
[5]**drown:** die because of being unable to take in air while underwater

The answer is easy to understand when you look at the seafood they catch. 60-year-old Song Ho has had a good day. The seafood she has caught may make up to 300 U.S. dollars!

Diving is still a big business in Cheju and divers can make a good living doing it. It used to be the only way the women could get food for their families. However, it now also gives them a chance to educate their children for a better life. So what about the next generation? What about the younger women of Cheju?

Divers can make up to 300 U.S. dollars on a good day!

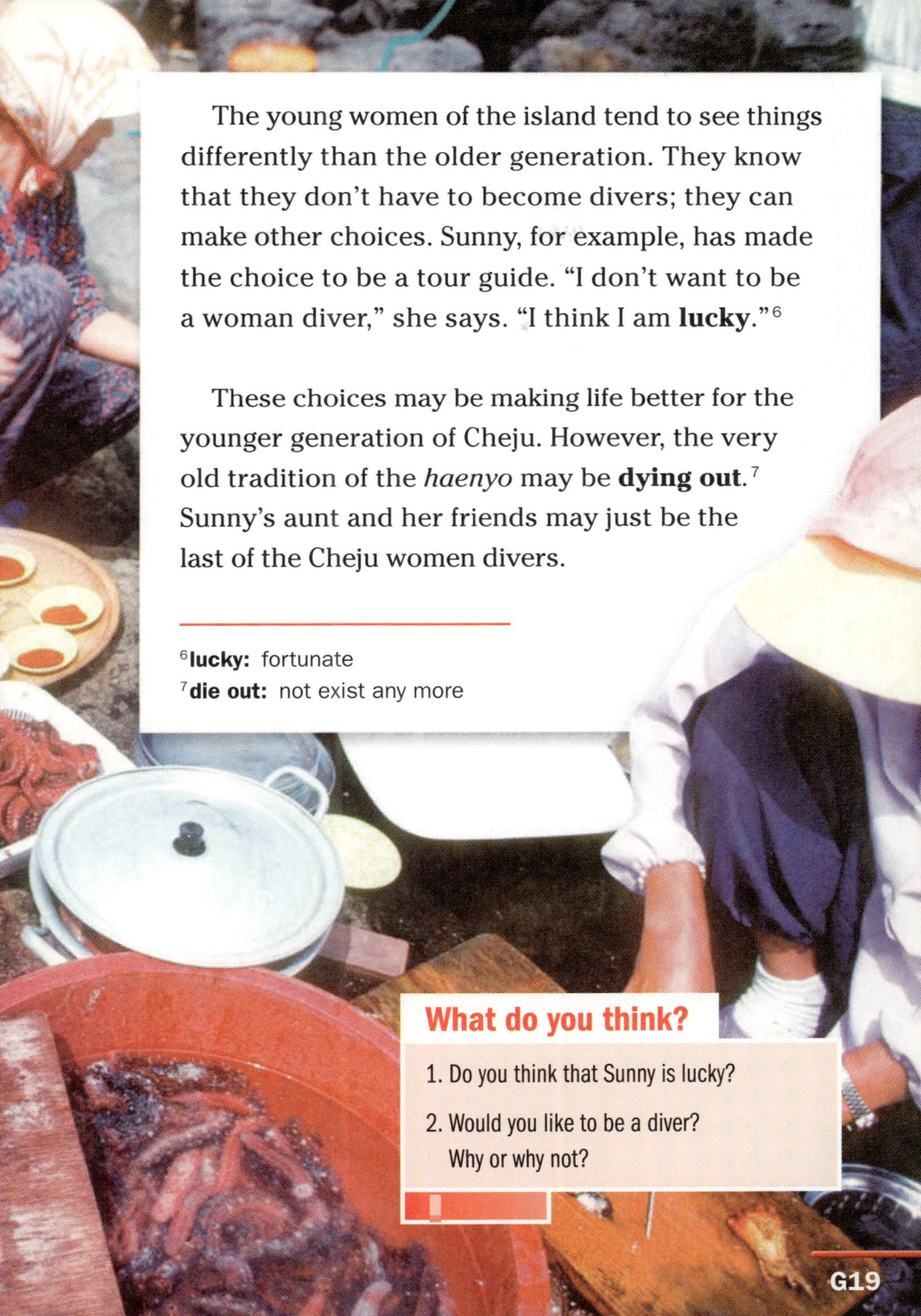

The young women of the island tend to see things differently than the older generation. They know that they don't have to become divers; they can make other choices. Sunny, for example, has made the choice to be a tour guide. "I don't want to be a woman diver," she says. "I think I am **lucky**."[6]

These choices may be making life better for the younger generation of Cheju. However, the very old tradition of the *haenyo* may be **dying out**.[7] Sunny's aunt and her friends may just be the last of the Cheju women divers.

---

[6]**lucky:** fortunate
[7]**die out:** not exist any more

What do you think?

1. Do you think that Sunny is lucky?
2. Would you like to be a diver? Why or why not?

After You Read

1. Women divers _____ the island of Cheju dive into the sea every day.
   A. off
   B. from
   C. for
   D. into

2. Which is NOT a good heading for page G7?
   A. Women Divers Catch Food for Island
   B. A History of the Cheju Divers
   C. The First Generation of Divers
   D. The Changing Lives of Women in Cheju

3. On page G7, 'they' in 'they catch' refers to:
   A. octopus, abalone, and sea urchin
   B. the young women in Cheju
   C. the people of Cheju
   D. the divers on the island

4. Why is Sunny Hong part of a new generation?
   A. She wants to be an English teacher.
   B. She has a different life.
   C. She has an aptitude for diving.
   D. all of the above

5. Why does the writer explain that Sunny taught herself English?
   A. to show that Sunny has decided to do something different
   B. to show that Sunny is the same as her family
   C. to show that Sunny is scared of the water
   D. to show that Sunny must be a diver

6. On page G11, what is the closest meaning of 'depend on'?
   A. use
   B. have
   C. need
   D. love

7. Choose the best heading for page G12.
   A. Women Choose to Be Divers
   B. Diving Safest Job on Island
   C. Village Women Choose Dangerous Jobs
   D. Diving Was the Only Option

8. Which is NOT a danger of diving?
   A. ears
   B. pains
   C. drowning
   D. death

9. In paragraph 1 on page G15, 'it' refers to:
   A. developing pains
   B. diving
   C. experiencing problems
   D. getting older

10. What do the *haenyos* probably think about diving?
    A. Diving is an easy way to make a living.
    B. Diving is a way to make a lot of money.
    C. Tour guides make more money.
    D. none of the above

11. How did women divers better educate their children?
    A. They taught them a lot about diving.
    B. They showed them how wonderful diving can be.
    C. They taught them how to sell seafood.
    D. They gave them money to go to school.

12. Sunny thinks she is lucky _____ she can make other choices.
    A. for
    B. who
    C. because
    D. where

A Diving Vacation!

Are you looking for a different kind of vacation?

Every year thousands of tourists visit Hawaii. Many of them stay in hotels on the Big Island. Others make a different choice. Here at Hawaii Vacations, we offer active vacations in Hawaii that are away from the majority of the tourists. We offer scuba diving vacations around this beautiful island. Our customers spend their vacations wearing oxygen tanks and diving deep into the ocean. They do this in order to look at beautiful fish and unusual plants. There are many places to dive in the Hawaiian Islands. One of the most special is Lanai Lookout on the island of O'ahu.

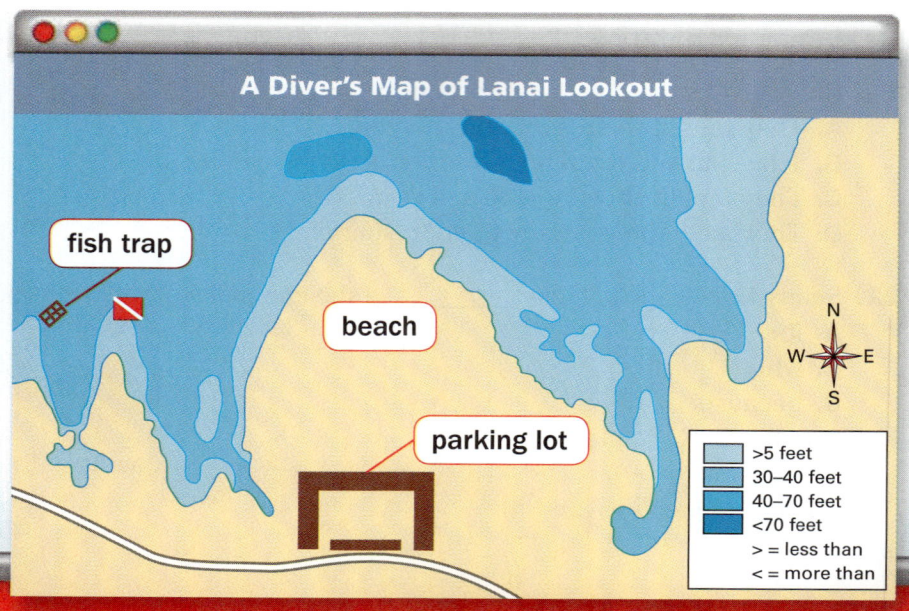

A Diver's Map of Lanai Lookout

- fish trap
- beach
- parking lot

>5 feet
30–40 feet
40–70 feet
<70 feet
> = less than
< = more than

A view from Lanai Lookout

Why should you visit O'ahu with Hawaii Vacations?

O'ahu is 150 miles north of the Big Island of Hawaii. It is home to Hawaii's biggest city, Honolulu. Our customers usually stay in Honolulu. We take them to visit the most attractive places where they can enjoy nature. Lanai Lookout is a favorite place for divers who want to experience the beauty of this island. We offer a special scuba diving visit to Lanai Lookout.

A Day at Lanai Lookout

Beginner divers are not allowed to dive here. We only take experienced divers because the ocean has very strong tides and currents. It can be dangerous for a beginner. Our visit to Lanai is an unforgettable experience. You begin by walking from the parking lot down to the ocean. Before starting your dive, our trainers will help you to check the map to see how deep the water is. Your first stop is the well-known fish trap. This is where Hawaii University catches fish for scientific studies. During the dive, our trainers will help you to stay safe. They will ensure that you stay in areas where the water is less than 40 feet deep. We promise you will love the beauty of Lanai Lookout and enjoy this special dive.

CD 2, Track 04

Word Count: 328
Time: _____

Vocabulary List

aptitude (G: 8)
aunt (G: 3, 11, 12, 19)
choice (G: 3, 12, 19)
die out (G: 19)
diver (G: 2, 3, 4, 7, 11, 12, 15, 17, 19)
drown (G: 15)
generation (G: 3, 7, 8, 15, 16, 19)
hold their breath (G: 4)
legendary (G: 3, 4)
lucky (G: 19)
make a living (G: 3, 7, 16)
ocean (G: 2, 8, 11, 15)
oxygen tank (G: 2, 4)
seafood (G: 2, 4, 7, 8, 16)
tides and currents (G: 15)
tour guide (G: 3, 8, 19)
tourist (G: 3, 8)
volcano (G: 4)

Peruvian WEAVERS

Rob Waring, *Series Editor*

Australia • Brazil • Japan • Korea • Mexico • Singapore • Spain • United Kingdom • United States

Words to Know

This story is set in Peru. It happens in a village in the Andes Mountains. The village is called Chinchero [tʃintʃɛroʊ] and it is near the city of Cuzco [kuskoʊ].

A **High in the Andes.** Read the definitions. Write the number of the correct underlined word next to each item in the picture.

1. Barley is a plant which produces small grains used for food and drink.
2. A sheep is an animal that farmers often raise for wool, meat, and milk.
3. A potato is a white root vegetable with brown, red, or yellow skin.
4. A llama is an animal that people often use to carry things in the Andes.
5. A farmer is a person who raises animals or plants for food.

Villagers in the Andes

B **Traditional Peruvian Weaving.** Read the paragraph. Then, match each word with the correct definition.

   This story is about a group of women weavers in a small village. These weavers use wool, or the hair from sheep and llamas, to make cloth. They do this by crossing pieces of yarn or other material over and under one another. This process is called weaving. The weavers make blankets for their beds and shawls to wear so they can stay warm. They also sell these items and use the money to help the local economy.

1. wool _____
2. cloth _____
3. yarn _____
4. weave _____
5. blanket _____
6. shawl _____

a. a material often used for making clothing
b. sheep or llama hair
c. a warm covering for the bed
d. a thin twisted fiber made of cotton, wool, etc.
e. an article of clothing worn around the shoulders
f. make cloth by crossing pieces of yarn over and under one another

Weaving Yarn into Cloth

In a small village high in the Andes, the weaving process starts with just one sheep. First, a few people from the village, or villagers, prepare the **knife.**[1] Then, they carefully tie up the sheep so that it can't move. Finally, they use the knife to cut the sheep's winter coat of wool. After that, one of the newest and most important industries in Chinchero begins.

---

[1]**knife:** a tool used to cut things

CD 2, Track 05

Cutting Wool from a Sheep with a Knife

The methods they use are traditional, but these villagers really are part of something new. The wool they're collecting is for a new and different kind of business in the village of Chinchero. It's for a weavers' **cooperative**[2] that the women here manage.

Every Monday and Saturday, 46 women and girls—all members of the cooperative—cut wool from their sheep and llamas. Then, they **spin**[3] the wool and work it into yarn. After that, they use the yarn to make cloth.

---

[2] **cooperative:** a business owned jointly with others
[3] **spin:** turn wool or another material into yarn

Nilda Cayanupa[4] is the leader of the Center for Traditional **Textiles**,[5] which manages the cooperative. She explains why she helped to start the cooperative: "[Not many people] of my age in my town [were] learning to weave. So it was kind of sad that weaving was disappearing. So, because [of] that, my dream was always that the younger **generation**[6] should learn [how to weave] so the weaving won't die."

Nilda and the cooperative are working to ensure that the traditional weaving of the Andes won't disappear.

---

[4]**Nilda Cayanupa:** [nɪldə kaɪənupə]
[5]**textile:** general term for cloth or things people weave
[6]**generation:** people of a similar age within a society or family

Nilda grew up in the Andean **countryside**,[7] where many of the men are farmers. According to Nilda, her village produces a lot of very good foods. "Chinchero is a farming village," she says. "We are the best—I'm not saying [this] because I am from this village—but we are the best producers of potatoes, and many things like **quinoa**[8] [and] barley."

---

[7] **countryside:** land in its natural condition that is not in a town or city
[8] **quinoa:** a plant grown for food and often eaten like rice

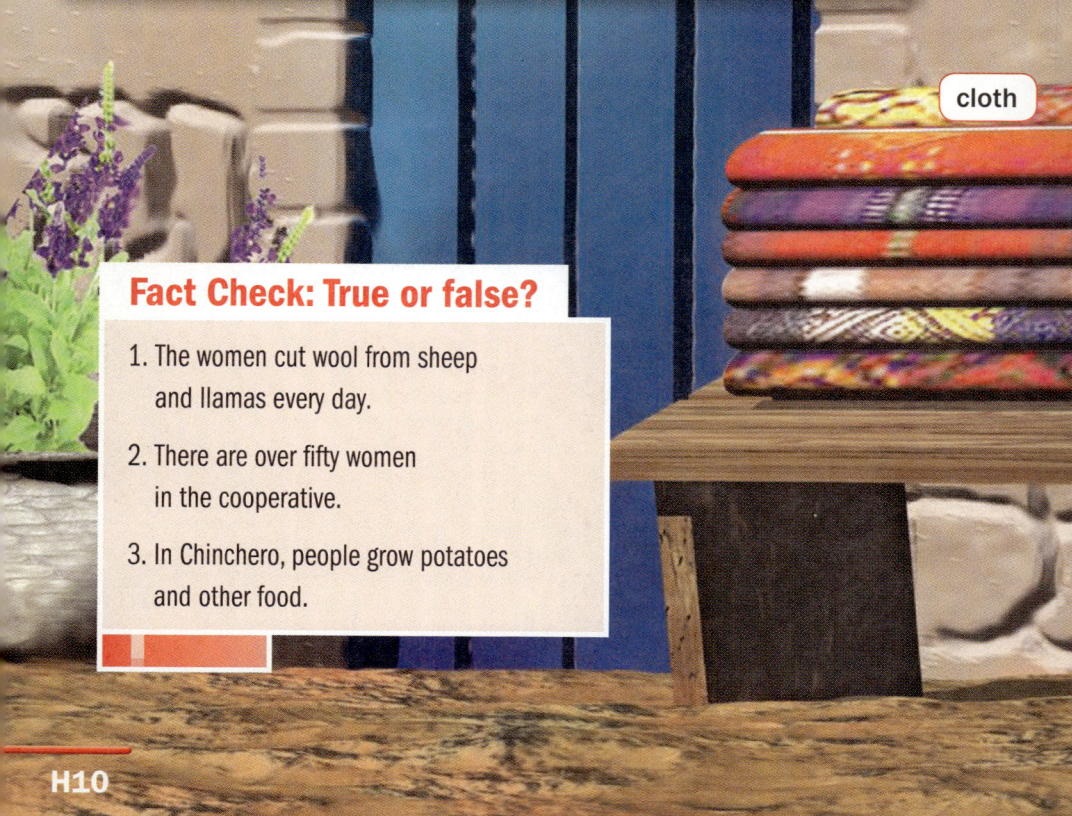

cloth

Fact Check: True or false?

1. The women cut wool from sheep and llamas every day.
2. There are over fifty women in the cooperative.
3. In Chinchero, people grow potatoes and other food.

Many products are made or grown in Chinchero.

Farming has long been a tradition in Chinchero. Many farmers here continue the traditions of the **Inca people**[9] who lived in the Andes for centuries.

However, the economy is changing. Farming no longer brings in enough money to support a whole family here. So, with the changes in the economy, traditional ideas are changing, too. Until now it's always been the men who have farmed. Traditionally, the women have cooked and cared for the children. They have also taken wool from the sheep and woven it into cloth. It's this weaving process that is now becoming more and more important.

---

[9]**Inca people:** South American group of people from long ago.

Nilda agrees that these women weavers are becoming more important. They're becoming the main economic supporters of the family. As an example, she tells of one woman whose husband has started helping with the sheep. She explains that this wasn't very common in the past. Until recently, the men only farmed the land and didn't help with the weaving. This is now changing because women can make a good amount of money with their weaving. Nilda says, "Today, this group of ladies can make … not a lot of money … but a reasonable amount of money."

Now in Chinchero, Peruvian weaving isn't just a tradition anymore. It's a way for these women to make money and live well.

Weaving has also become more important for the culture of Chinchero. It has become a way to make the textile tradition stronger and to keep a part of the past alive. One older weaver talks about how she learned how to weave: "I learned when I was in the third grade of school with very basic weaving," she says. "Today, I weave blankets, shawls, **ponchos,**[10] and prepare my own yarn."

The older women here are now teaching the younger girls. The goal is to bring back the strength of the textile tradition of the past. They want to keep the Peruvian weaving traditions alive.

---

[10] **poncho:** a piece of clothing shaped like a blanket with a hole for the head

As the young women of Chinchero learn to weave, they also learn to be **self-sufficient.**[11] They can sell the blankets and clothes that they make in their free time. "I do my weaving in my house, in the afternoons and the early morning," explains one young girl. "And [at the cooperative] on Monday and Saturday, too," she adds.

Weaving groups like the Chinchero cooperative are giving new life to the textile tradition. In the end, their cooperative may prove that many **threads**[12] together are stronger than one alone.

---

[11]**self-sufficient:** financially independent; able to live without help from others
[12]**threads:** long, thin pieces of wool or cotton used in weaving; a very thin form of yarn

Infer Meaning

1. What does the writer mean by the last sentence?
2. What makes you think that?

After You Read

1. What is the writer's purpose on page H4?
   A. to introduce the weaving industry of Chinchero
   B. to show what happens to sheep in Chinchero
   C. to introduce the Colombian countryside
   D. to show a sheep after winter

2. On page H4, what does 'industries' mean?
   A. farming methods
   B. artist communities
   C. business activities
   D. ways of cutting wool

3. According to page H7, why are the women weavers part of something new?
   A. They've made a new community for weaving and selling.
   B. They've developed a new style of collecting wool.
   C. The women are managing a new kind of village.
   D. Their wool is new and different.

4. In paragraph 1 on page H7, 'they' refers to:
   A. fifty women and girls
   B. the sheep and llamas
   C. wool cutters
   D. cooperative members

5. A good heading for page H8 is:
   A. Center for Traditional Textiles Unsuccessful
   B. Weaving Disappears from Andes
   C. Woman Has Dream to Help Traditional Weaving
   D. Younger Generation Starts Textile Cooperative

6. Which item does NOT come from the Andean countryside?
   A. tomatoes
   B. barley
   C. potatoes
   D. quinoa

7. On page H10, the word 'produces' can be replaced by:
   A. sells
   B. grows
   C. buys
   D. contains

8. How is the economy changing in Chinchero?
   A. Farming is becoming stronger.
   B. Men are starting to weave.
   C. Women are making money from weaving.
   D. Families are farming together.

9. Weaving is a way _____ women to support their families.
   A. to
   B. for
   C. as
   D. in

10. Which is NOT a good heading for page H14?
   A. Money from Weaving Is Reasonable
   B. Husbands Help with Sheep
   C. The Past Was a Different Time
   D. Men Don't Like New Life

11. In paragraph 2 on page H17, who is 'they'?
   A. the older weavers
   B. the young women
   C. the men of the village
   D. the families

12. On page H18, what does the young girl probably think about weaving?
   A. Weaving is tiring and takes a lot of time.
   B. Weaving is something her family can do together.
   C. Weaving is easy for her to do in different places.
   D. Weaving is impossible without the cooperative.

Foods of
THE WORLD

As part of our series on 'Foods of the World', reporter Ana Ruiz met traveler and food writer Monica Mason. Monica has just returned from South America where she was studying traditional foods of the Inca. Read on to discover what interesting facts she uncovered.

Quinoa

Q: WHY DID YOU DECIDE TO GO TO PERU?

A: My aim was to learn as much as I could about the traditional foods of the Inca people. I spent some time with families in small villages in the mountains. I wanted to see what foods they ate. I had a feeling that some of the 'modern' foods that we eat today are actually traditional foods.

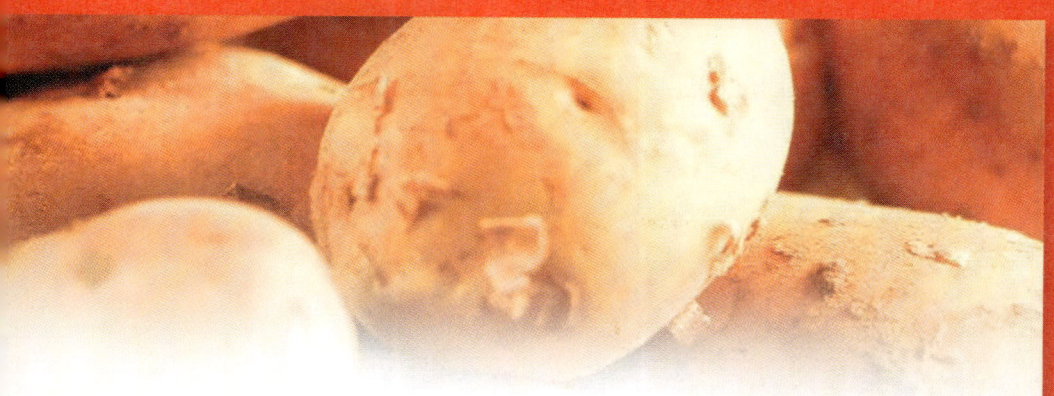

Q: WHAT DID YOU LEARN?

A: I was correct! Recently, doctors have told people to eat quinoa to be healthy. But quinoa was actually often used in traditional Inca foods. It was even more common than the potato. This was because quinoa was easy to grow in dry areas near the tops of mountains. That's where a lot of the people lived.

Q WHAT ELSE DID THEY EAT?

A: The Inca ate a lot of potatoes as well, but they weren't as important as quinoa. Most people have always been able to get potatoes. However, it's only in the past twenty years that we can buy the healthier quinoa. I find that a bit strange!

Q: WHAT WAS THE MOST INTERESTING THING YOU LEARNED ABOUT THE INCA?

A: One interesting thing is that they had a method of storing potatoes for long periods of time. When the weather became very cold, they would place potatoes in the ground all night. This caused them to become very cold and hard, or 'freeze.' During the day, the Inca would put the potatoes near a hot fire. This combination of hot and cold caused the potatoes to dry out. Once they were dry, they could keep the potatoes for a long time.

🎧 **CD 2, Track 06**

Word Count: 322
Time: _____

Vocabulary List

barley (H: 2, 10, 11)
blanket (H: 3, 11, 17, 18)
cloth (H: 3, 7, 8, 11, 17, 18)
cooperative (H: 7, 8, 10, 18)
countryside (H: 10)
disappear (H: 8)
farmer (H: 2, 10, 13)
knife (H: 4)
llama (H: 2, 3, 7, 10)
poncho (H: 17)
potato (H: 2, 10, 11)
quinoa (H: 10)
self-sufficient (H: 18)
shawl (H: 3, 11, 17)
sheep (H: 2, 3, 4, 5, 7, 10, 13, 14)
spin (H: 7)
textile (H: 8, 17, 18)
thread (H: 18)
weave (H: 3, 4, 7, 8, 13, 14, 17, 18)
wool (H: 3, 4, 5, 7, 10, 11, 13, 18)
yarn (H: 3, 7, 11, 17, 18)

Taiko MASTER

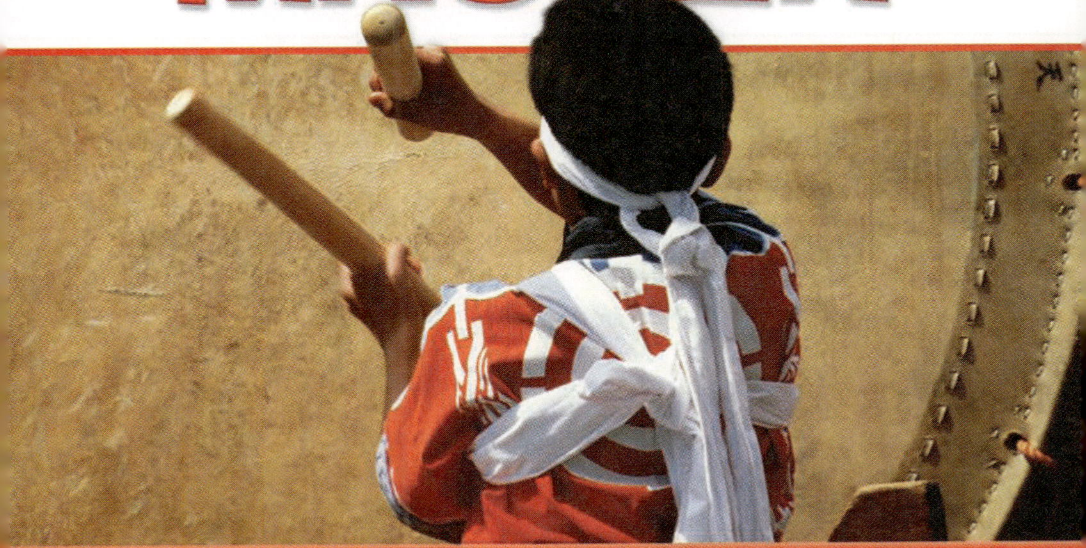

Rob Waring, *Series Editor*

Australia • Brazil • Japan • Korea • Mexico • Singapore • Spain • United Kingdom • United States

Words to Know

This story is set in the United States (U.S.). It happens in San Francisco [sæn frənsɪskoʊ], California, near the Pacific Ocean.

A **Taiko Drumming.** Read the paragraph. Then, match each word with the correct definition.

Taiko drumming is an ancient Japanese art, but it is also done in Western countries. 'Taiko' is a Japanese word which means 'drum.' These musical instruments make loud noises when taiko drummers beat them. They use drumsticks to do this. Taiko drumming is difficult and the drummers must practice so they can improve. They practice in a special place called a 'dojo.' If a person works very hard, he or she may become a grand master of taiko.

1. drum _____
2. beat _____
3. drumstick _____
4. practice _____
5. *dojo* _____
6. grand master _____

a. hit again and again
b. a stick for hitting a drum
c. someone who performs an art at the highest level
d. a Japanese word for 'practice place'
e. do something again and again to get better at it
f. a round musical instrument hit with hands or sticks

Taiko Drummers

B In the *Dojo*.
Read the definitions. Complete the paragraph with the correct form of the words.

mind: the part of a person that allows them to think and feel
sensei: Japanese word which means 'teacher'
warrior: fighter
traditional: done for a long time by a particular society or group

Many Japanese arts are practiced in a 'dojo.' A *dojo* is a place where people can practice (1)_____ Japanese arts. *Dojos* have a long history. They are the places where many strong Japanese (2)_____ practiced and became very good fighters. In a *dojo*, there is always a (3)_____, or teacher, who helps the students improve. The students have to work hard with both their bodies and their (4)_____.

Warriors Fighting in an Ancient Dojo

Two thousand years ago, Japanese warriors used drums to make their **enemies**[1] fear them. In ancient Japan, the drum was very important in everyday life, too. People used to mark village **boundaries**[2] by how far the sounds of drums traveled. People even used to do their daily activities to the beat of drums. However, slowly over the years, the sound of the drums went away—until now.

---

[1] **enemy:** a person or group that wants to hurt another
[2] **boundary:** the point where one thing ends and another begins

 CD 2, Track 07

Japanese warriors used drums to make their enemies afraid.

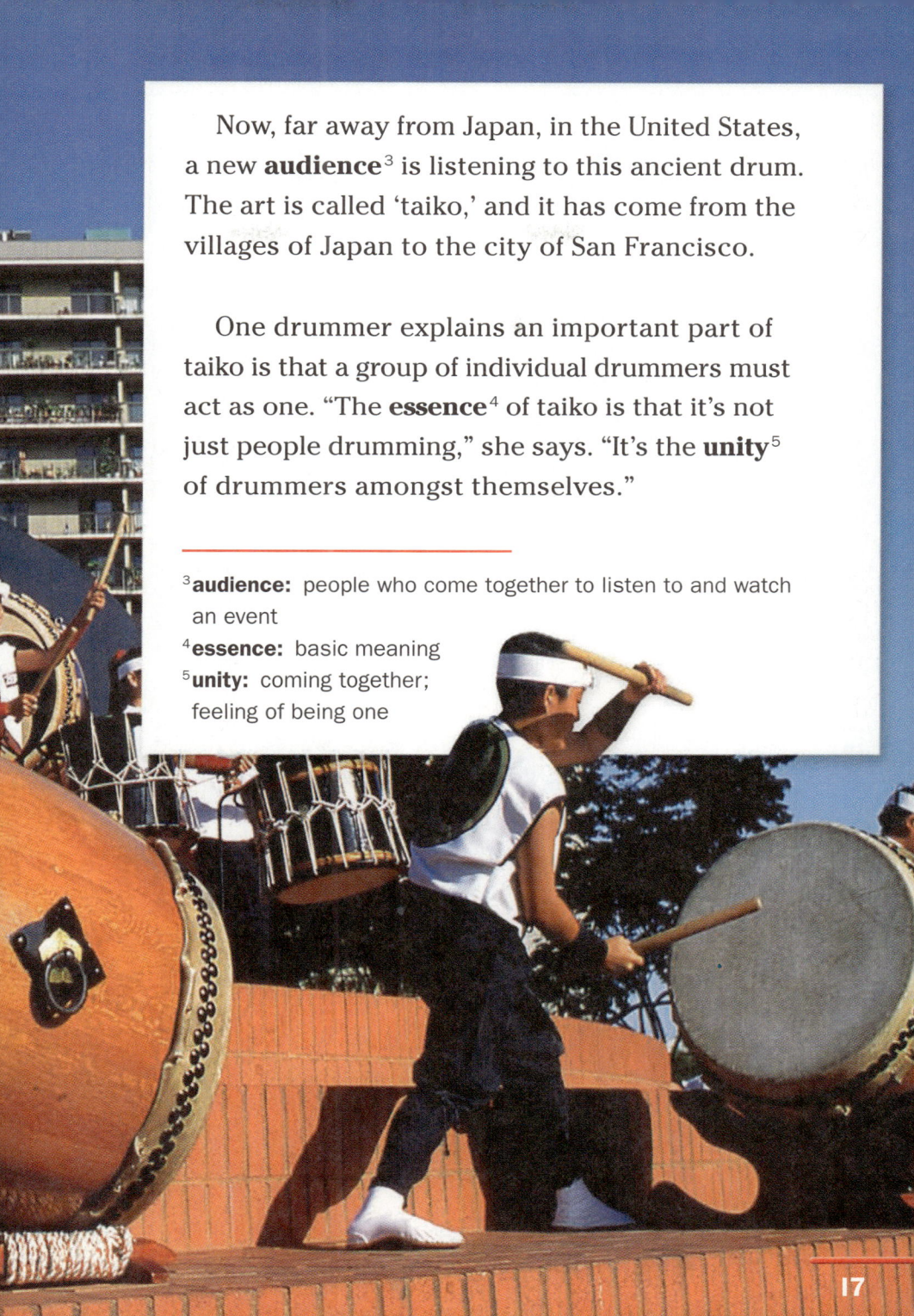

Now, far away from Japan, in the United States, a new **audience**[3] is listening to this ancient drum. The art is called 'taiko,' and it has come from the villages of Japan to the city of San Francisco.

One drummer explains an important part of taiko is that a group of individual drummers must act as one. "The **essence**[4] of taiko is that it's not just people drumming," she says. "It's the **unity**[5] of drummers amongst themselves."

---

[3]**audience:** people who come together to listen to and watch an event
[4]**essence:** basic meaning
[5]**unity:** coming together; feeling of being one

In San Francisco, the movement of the body has now been added to traditional taiko drumming. It is now an art form that brings together sound, body, and mind. During a performance, the energy of all of these parts goes into the beating of the drums.

Identify the Main Idea

1. What is the main idea of the paragraph?
2. What would be a better heading for this page?
   a. 'Traditional Taiko Drumming'
   b. 'Taiko Combines Sound, Body, and Mind'

Some ancient arts have added body movement to bring together sound, body and mind.

Taiko Grand Master Seiichi Tanaka explains what happens when the drummer and drum unite. According to him, it's almost as if the drum and drummer become one. "Your self and the drum, totally get together. Into the drum, your self," he says as he moves his body forward, "… and [the] drum [comes] to you," he adds as he moves his body back. "Both [are] **mutual**,[7]" he explains.

---

[7] **mutual:** equal or similar

Scan for Information

Scan pages 112-115 to find the information.

1. When did Seiichi Tanaka come to the U.S.?

2. In which two countries did Seiichi Tanaka start taiko drumming?

3. How many groups in the two countries are there now?

In the early 1900s, traditional taiko was very popular in Japanese-American communities. However, by the mid 1900s, many people were losing interest in taiko drumming. Then, in 1968, Seiichi Tanaka arrived and brought a new interest and a new style of drumming from Japan. After that, things changed. Tanaka explains: "I was just **fresh off the boat**,"[8] he says, "so [a] whole bunch of 'fresh off the boat' people [got] together and play[ed] drums."

---

[8]**fresh off the boat:** *(slang)* new to a place or experience

Tanaka is also known as 'Tanaka Sensei' to his students in the *dojo*. They know that he is an important man in taiko. They also realize that he is responsible in part for its popularity in North America. "Tanaka Sensei is a real **pioneer**,"[9] says one student. "He's made a **dozen**[10] or so groups in the sixties and seventies, into something like eight hundred groups now spread all over this country and Canada."

---

[9] **pioneer:** one of the first people to do something
[10] **dozen:** twelve of something

What makes taiko special? According to Tanaka Sensei and other taiko drummers, it's all about the feeling of energy. "All energy from **Mother Nature**[11] [goes] through your body, come[s] to my body—here" Tanaka says, pointing to his arm. He then adds, "[it] go[es] through to the drumstick—BAM!" he says, as he moves his drumstick quickly.

One student explains that taiko drummers sometimes have to play through pain and tiredness while practicing or performing. At that point, he says that they can really express their feelings and energy. According to him, "it's almost as if you are standing outside of your body kind of looking in…and you hit this point where you're just completely free."

---

[11] **Mother Nature:** the imaginary mother of all things

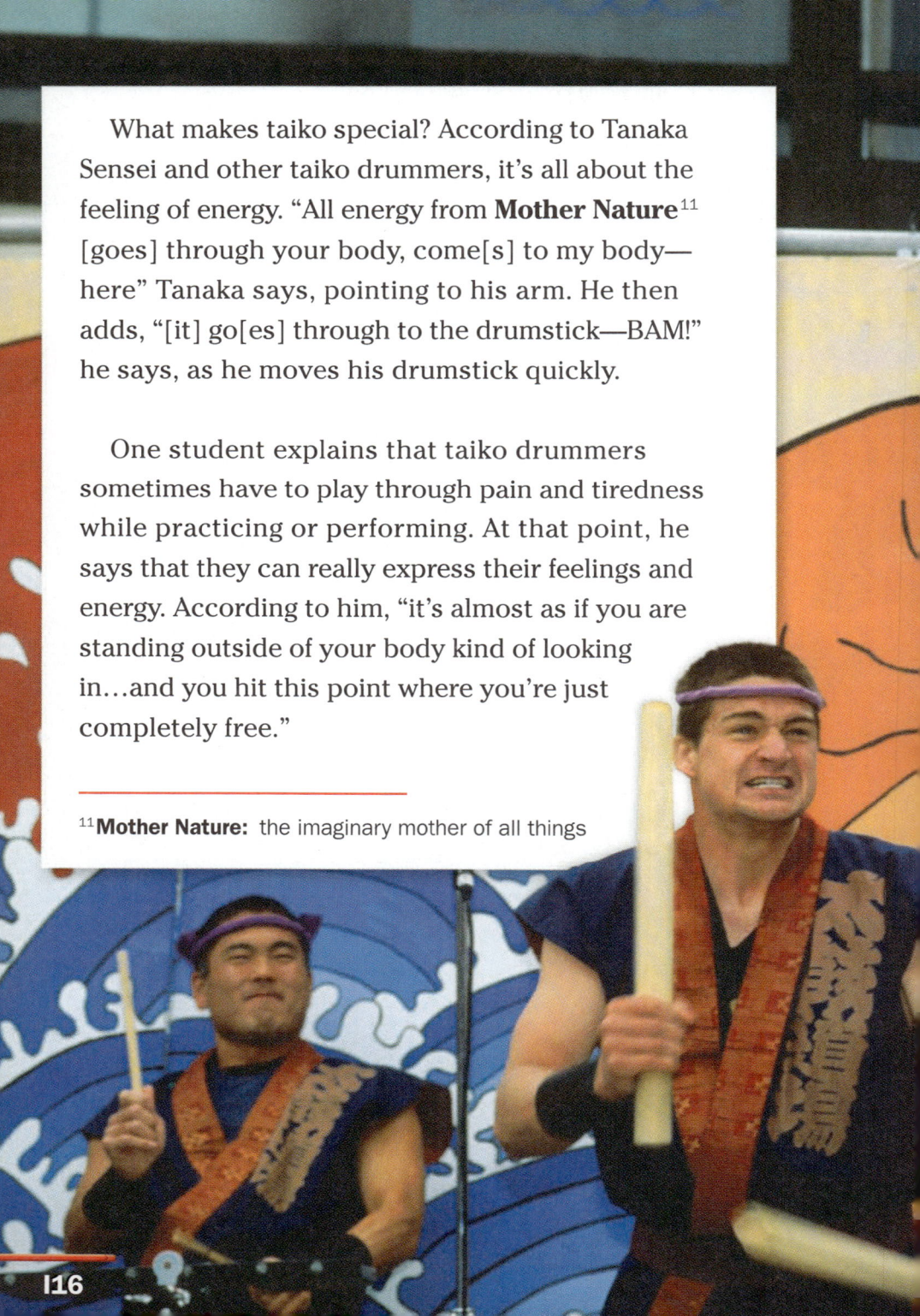

Another drummer also feels that taiko is about giving energy. "The essence of taiko is giving your 110 percent," she says. "You have to always give, because if you don't give, and everyone else is giving, then you're **draining**[12] from them."

Here in San Francisco, taiko came from the old world of Japan and was born again. Grand Master Seiichi Tanaka has given North America the chance to enjoy the energy and excitement of traditional taiko drumming.

---

[12] **drain:** take away; use up

After You Read

1. Japanese warriors used their drums to make their enemies _____.
   A. dance
   B. fight
   C. afraid
   D. find

2. On page I4, the word 'mark' can be replaced by:
   A. touch
   B. stop
   C. research
   D. show

3. On page I7, the drummer believes that an important part of taiko is the:
   A. group experience
   B. individual drummers
   C. basic meaning
   D. audience

4. According to page I8, taiko brings what things together:
   A. sound, body and mind
   B. energy, body and tradition
   C. art, sound and body
   D. drums, performance and tradition

5. On page I8, 'it' refers to:
   A. movement
   B. sound
   C. taiko
   D. a city

6. What is a good heading for page I11?
   A. Taiko Drums Sound Important
   B. Unity of the Drum and Drummer
   C. Body and Self are Mutual
   D. Drummers Climb into Drums

7. According to Tanaka, how do the drummer and drum become one?
   A. The energy of playing brings them together.
   B. The drum touches the drummer.
   C. The drummer unites with other drums.
   D. The movement brings together all drummers.

8. What's a good heading for page I12?
   A. Japan's Drumming on the Boat
   B. Traditional Taiko Comes from U.S.
   C. Tanaka Brings New Drumming Style
   D. Fresh Off the Boat in 1900

9. On page I15, 'sixties and seventies' refers to:
   A. the number of drummers
   B. the time between 1960 and 1979
   C. Tanaka's age
   D. the number of drums

10. Tanaka Sensei thinks that drumming is special because of the:
   A. energy
   B. drumsticks
   C. sound 'BAM!'
   D. taiko drums

11. For taiko drummers, the feeling of _____ sometimes comes after pain and tiredness.
   A. playing
   B. draining
   C. freedom
   D. outside

12. What is the main purpose of this story?
   A. to explain the phrase of 'grand master'
   B. to talk to many drummers about taiko
   C. to compare old and new Japan
   D. to introduce an energetic drumming style

Scotland's African Drum Village

Most people think of Scotland as a quiet place with fields and farm animals. But did you know that Scotland has a lot more to offer? In recent years, Dundee, Scotland's fourth-largest city, has become a center for the arts. Few people think of Scotland as a place to hear African drumming. However, just north of Dundee, there is an African drumming program that attracts a large audience. People come to this event from all over the world.

African Drum Village is a five-day meeting between drummers and people who enjoy the excitement of drumming. It is the first and only meeting of its kind in Scotland. Some of the best drummers

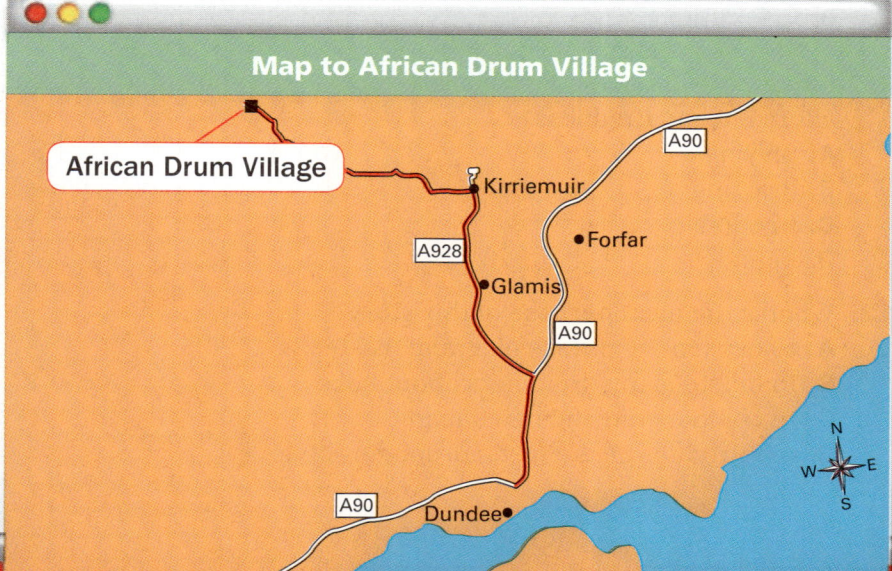

in the world attend the program. There is something for everyone at African Drum Village. As a visitor, you can listen to wonderful performances from grand masters. Beginners can also have drumming lessons with the masters. More experienced drummers can form drumming groups with others. African Drum Village is a spiritual event for many visitors. It is their chance to connect with nature and discover new music. The beauty of Scotland and the skill of the drummers ensure that visitors have a wonderful experience.

This year musician and teacher Famoudou Konaté is the main attraction at African Drum Village. Mr. Konaté is a grand master of drumming in the ancient Malinké Djembe tradition. He was born in 1940 in the country of Guinea in Africa. By the time he was 14 years old, his drumming was already well known throughout Africa. For the last 40 years, Konaté has performed in Europe, the United States, and many other parts of the world. African Drum Village is very pleased to present Mr. Konaté this year.

A Visitor Enjoying African Drum Village

CD 2, Track 08

Word Count: 329
Time: _____

Vocabulary List

audience (l: 7)
beat (l: 2, 4, 8)
boundary (l: 4)
dojo (l: 2, 3, 15)
dozen (l: 15)
drain (l: 19)
drum (l: 2, 4, 5, 7, 8, 11, 12, 16, 19)
drumstick (l: 2, 16)
enemy (l: 4)
essence (l: 7, 19)
fresh off the boat (l: 12)
grand master (l: 2, 11, 19)
mind (l: 3, 8, 9)
Mother Nature (l: 16)
mutual (l: 11)
pioneer (l: 15)
practice (l: 2, 3, 16)
sensei (l: 3, 15)
traditional (l: 3, 8, 12)
unity (l: 7)
warrior (l: 3, 4, 5)

Cheese-Rolling RACES

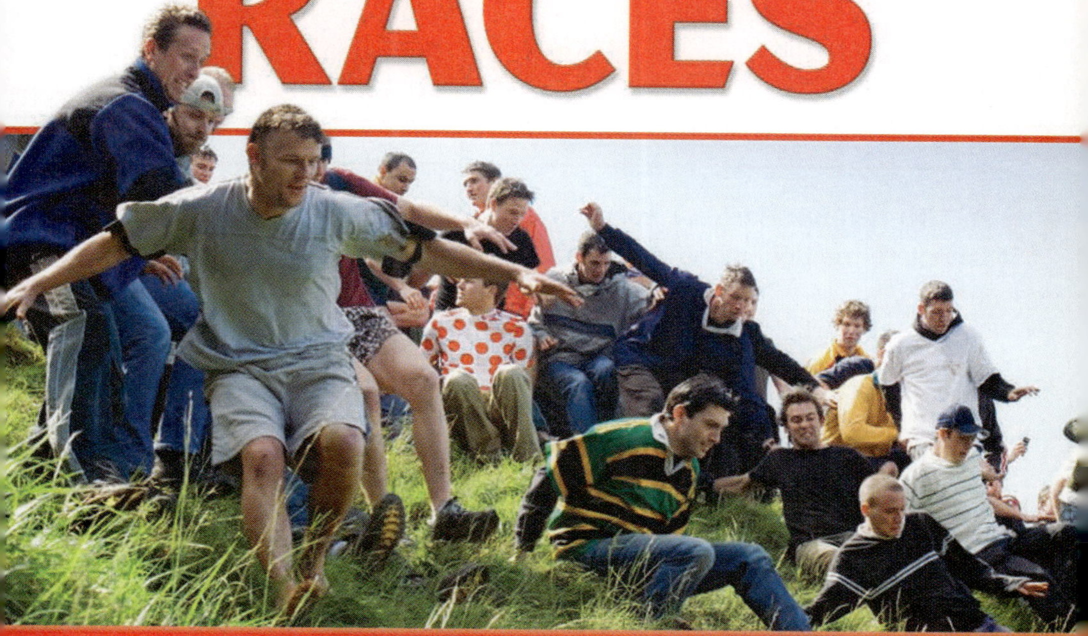

Rob Waring, *Series Editor*

Australia • Brazil • Japan • Korea • Mexico • Singapore • Spain • United Kingdom • United States

Words to Know

This story is set in England, in the United Kingdom. It happens in the town of Brockworth [brɒkwɜrθ].

A **At the Races.** Here are some words you will see in the story. Complete the definitions with words in the box.

| cheer | prize | route |
| crowd | race | spectators |

1. The road or way you follow to get from one place to another place is a _____.
2. An event in which people try to be the fastest to do something is a _____.
3. To shout loudly to encourage someone is to _____.
4. A large group of people is a _____.
5. _____ are the people who are watching a sporting event, show, etc.
6. A _____ is something that is given to someone who wins a competition.

B Cheese-Rolling Races.
Read the paragraph and look at the picture. Then match each word to the correct definition.

In England, many towns have traditional competitions. In them, competitors usually try to win a game or contest. However, the annual cheese-rolling race in Brockworth is a little unusual. At the start of the race, someone rolls a wheel of cheese down a very steep hill. Then, the competitors run after the cheese. The first person to reach the bottom of the hill is the winner.

1. competition _____
2. competitor _____
3. annual _____
4. roll _____
5. wheel of cheese _____
6. steep _____

a. going up or down very suddenly
b. move quickly in a circular motion
c. person who takes part in a race or contest
d. one time every year
e. a large, round piece of cheese
f. an organized event in which people try to be the best or fastest

The Annual Cheese-Rolling Race

Cheese-rolling has been a tradition in the town of Brockworth since the early 1800s. But what happens in this old and locally famous competition? It's quite simple, really. First, the competitors come together at the top of a hill named 'Cooper's Hill.' The **slope**[1] of the hill is very steep—almost 45 degrees! And after that? They wait, but wait for what?

---

[1]**slope:** the amount of difference between a high area and a lower area

CD 2, Track 09

Cooper's Hill has a very steep slope!

What's the Main Idea?

1. What is the main idea of the paragraph on page J7?

2. How does the cheese-rolling competition work?

They wait for someone to push a very large wheel of cheese down the hill. The competitors then run very quickly after it. The cheese may reach up to **40 miles**[2] per hour. The competitors go pretty fast, too! The first one to the bottom of the hill wins. What's the prize for such an unusual event? It's the wheel of cheese—of course!

---

[2]**40 miles:** 64.3 kilometers

The first winner of the day in this year's competition is Craig Brown, a **pub**[3] worker. He's happy to be the winner, but he's also very tired. What did he do to win the race? Craig says that his plan was simple; the most important thing is just to continue running. "Keep [on] going," he says, "and try to get your **balance**[4] back." He then adds, "It's steeper than you could ever think. You'd have to run down there to really believe how steep it is!"

---

[3]**pub:** place where drinks and food are served
[4]**balance:** ability to stand up and not fall over due to unequal weight

Many people enjoy the cheese-rolling races of Brockworth. However, the race can be dangerous. You never know the route the cheese will take as it rolls down the hill. A few years ago, 30 people were **injured**[5] in an **accident**[6] at a race. One of the cheeses rolled down the hill too quickly and suddenly went into the crowd. Some of the spectators were hit by the cheese. Now, the competition route has **crash barriers.**[7] They protect the crowd from the cheese—and from the competitors!

[5]**injure:** cause bodily harm to a person or animal
[6]**accident:** a bad thing which happens without warning
[7]**crash barrier:** short wall along a competition route to protect spectators

Crash barriers protect the spectators at the races.

It's not just the spectators who get injured, the competitors do as well. This is especially true when the weather is very cold. There are also more injuries when there hasn't been much rain before the race. One organizer for the event explains, "It's when the ground is really hard … that's when the injuries are going to happen."

But the hard ground doesn't seem to stop the competitors. Every year there are a lot of people who follow Craig Brown's suggestion; they just 'keep on going' down Cooper's Hill. But what about Craig? How did he do in the remaining cheese-rolling races?

Well, Craig's plan to just 'keep on going' unfortunately failed. When he tried to keep on going in the second race, he lost his balance and fell—again and again! At the time, he was trying to get the competition's version of a 'double play'. He wanted to win two cheese wheels in one day. But instead of going home with a 'double cheese,' Craig went home with only one cheese, and maybe a few **bruises**![8]

---

[8]**bruises:** dark purple or black marks on the skin from an injury

So, what drives these runners? What makes them do it? Are they **crazy**?[9] One cheese runner thinks they may be. "It is dangerous," he says as he looks at the very steep slope of Cooper's Hill. "If I'm running down [the hill], [I] must be crazy. Yeah, I must be crazy … " he decides with a smile.

---

[9]**crazy:** not having a good mind; not sensible

The cheese racers of Brockworth may just be crazy. However, the crowds keep on cheering, and the competitors keep on running—year after year. It seems that a lot of people are very happy to try this dangerous run. Is it for the **fame**?[10] Is it for the fun? We may never know, but you can almost be sure of one thing; it's not only for the prize. It's more than just cheese that makes people want to win Brockworth's annual cheese-rolling race!

---

[10]**fame:** being known for one's achievements or skills

What do you think?

1. Do you think the cheese runners are crazy?

2. Would you like to be a competitor in this cheese-rolling competition? Why or why not?

3. Do you participate in any activities which other people might think are 'crazy'?

After You Read

1. On page J4, what does 'locally' mean?
   A. traditional
   B. in the area
   C. ancient
   D. totally

2. How long has the competition been happening?
   A. forty-five years
   B. less than two hundred years
   C. over two hundred years
   D. 1800 years

3. What is the goal of the competition?
   A. to be the first person down the hill
   B. to follow the competitors
   C. to be quicker than the cheese
   D. to roll cheese down a hill

4. On page J7, 'one' refers to a:
   A. wheel of cheese
   B. prize
   C. winner
   D. person

5. Choose the best heading for page J8.
   A. Tired But Happy Loser
   B. Hill Is Not So Bad
   C. Pub Worker Gets Cheese
   D. Balance Is Unimportant

6. How does Craig Brown describe the competition?
   A. simple, but steep
   B. unbelievably tiring
   C. harder than it looks
   D. easy if you don't stop

7. On page J10, 'it' is referring to the:
   A. race
   B. route
   C. cheese
   D. danger

8. One time the cheese crashed _____ a crowd of spectators.
   A. on
   B. in
   C. with
   D. into

9. When are injuries likely to occur during the races?
   A. if the weather is warm
   B. if the ground is too hard
   C. if it has rained before the race
   D. all of the above

10. What happens to Craig Brown in the second race?
    A. He loses his balance.
    B. He gets a double play.
    C. He wins the cheese.
    D. He is badly injured.

11. What's the purpose of page J16?
    A. to prove that the competition is safe
    B. to show the competitors are unhappy
    C. to prove that the town is crazy
    D. none of the above

12. What does the writer probably think about the competition?
    A. The spectators cheer too much.
    B. The race is too dangerous.
    C. The competitors like the fame and fun.
    D. The prize is very good cheese.

Bed Racing
It Isn't Crazy After All

Bed racing is becoming more popular in certain areas of the U.S. A bed race is a competition where teams of people push beds along a specific route. The route often goes through the middle of a city or town. The competing teams attempt to roll their beds along the route faster than anyone else. However, these are not just any beds! Racing beds often have very big wheels and the competitors sometimes paint them in some very interesting ways.

Most bed races are about having fun and raising money for the community.

2007 Race Results

	1st Place	2nd Place	3rd Place	Last Place
Team	Sleepwalkers	Morning Suns	Fast Times	Sleeping Beauties
Time	4 minutes, 31 seconds	4 minutes, 42 seconds	5 minutes, 10 seconds	14 minutes, 14 seconds

The teams build their own beds and practice for weeks before the race. However, race organizers often have firm rules about building and racing beds. For example: the beds must be a certain size, they can't have an engine, and they must have four wheels. In addition, there must be no more than six people pushing the bed and only one person can sit in the bed.

As long as the teams follow the rules, they can use their imaginations for everything else. Some beds are covered with flowers. Other beds look like crazy boats. To add to the fun, people often wear strange and unusual clothing.

On race days, large crowds of spectators come to cheer for their favorite team. These members of the community usually give money to their favorite team. However, the money doesn't go to the team members. It goes to organizations that help people in need. In the past, bed races have raised lots of money to provide health care for children and to help homeless people. At the end of the race, teams are often listed in a chart like the one above. Most of these teams don't even get a prize for winning. These bed races are obviously not serious events. The important thing is to raise money for the community and to have fun.

CD 2, Track 10

Word Count: 312
Time: _____

Vocabulary List

accident (J: 10)
annual (J: 3, 18)
balance (J: 8, 15)
bruise (J: 15)
cheer (J: 2, 18)
competition (J: 3, 4, 6, 7, 10, 15, 19)
competitor (J: 3, 4, 7, 10, 12, 18, 19)
crash barrier (J: 10)
crazy (J: 16, 18, 19)
crowd (J: 2, 10, 18)
fame (J: 18)
injure (J: 10, 12)
prize (J: 2, 7, 18)
pub (J: 8)
race (J: 2, 3, 8, 10)
roll (J: 3, 4, 6, 10, 12, 18, 19)
route (J: 2, 10)
slope (J: 4, 5, 16)
spectator (J: 2, 10, 12)
steep (J: 3, 4, 8, 16)
wheel of cheese (J: 3, 7, 15)

Making a Thai Boxing Champion

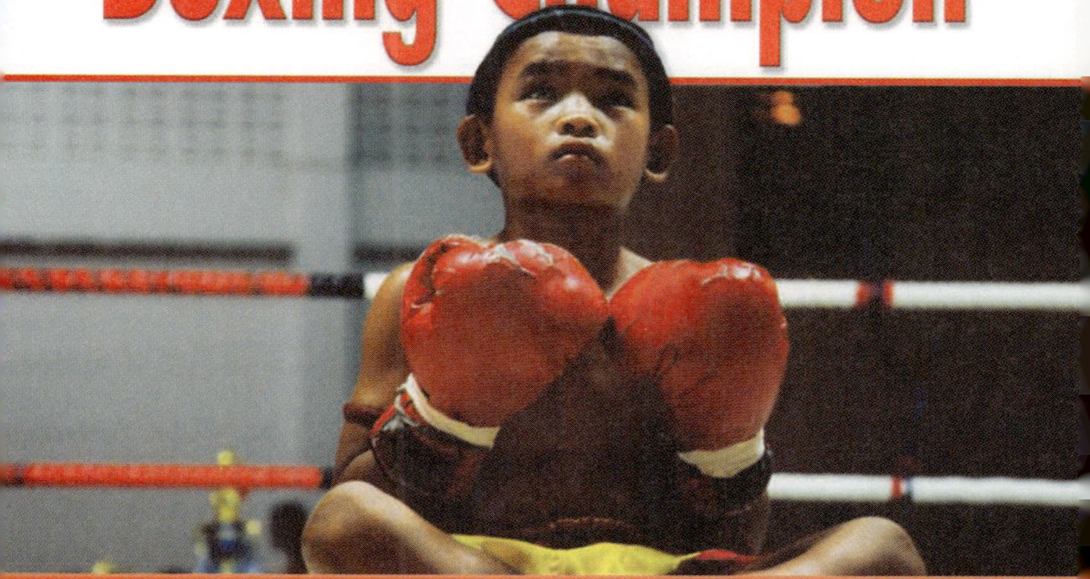

Rob Waring, *Series Editor*

Australia • Brazil • Japan • Korea • Mexico • Singapore • Spain • United Kingdom • United States

Words to Know

This story is set in Thailand. It happens in and around Chiang Mai [tʃæŋ maɪ], a city in the north of Thailand.

A **Thai Boxing.** Read the paragraph. Complete the definitions with the correct form of the underlined words.

Thai boxing, or *Muay Thai* [mu̯aɪ taɪ], is a traditional martial art from Thailand. It involves a number of special ceremonies. The boxers perform most of these special actions in the boxing ring. Thai boxers start training when they are very young. They all dream of becoming a champion. Being a Thai boxer gives them a high status in their community. It also makes their families very proud.

1. The _____ is the place where a fight happens.
2. _____ are people who fight for sport.
3. _____ means a special position in society.
4. _____ means pleased or satisfied with a person or action.
5. _____ are events or actions performed on special occasions.
6. The _____ are the traditional Asian skills of fighting.
7. A _____ is the final winner; the best.

Thai Boxers in the Boxing Ring

B Fighting with the Entire Body.
All of these body parts are used in Thai boxing. Read the definitions. Write the number of the correct underlined word next to each part of the body.

1. The knee is part of the leg. It connects the top of the leg to the bottom of the leg.
2. The elbow is part of the arm. It connects the two parts of the arm.
3. The head is at the top of the body.
4. The feet are at the ends of the legs.
5. The hands are at the ends of the arms.

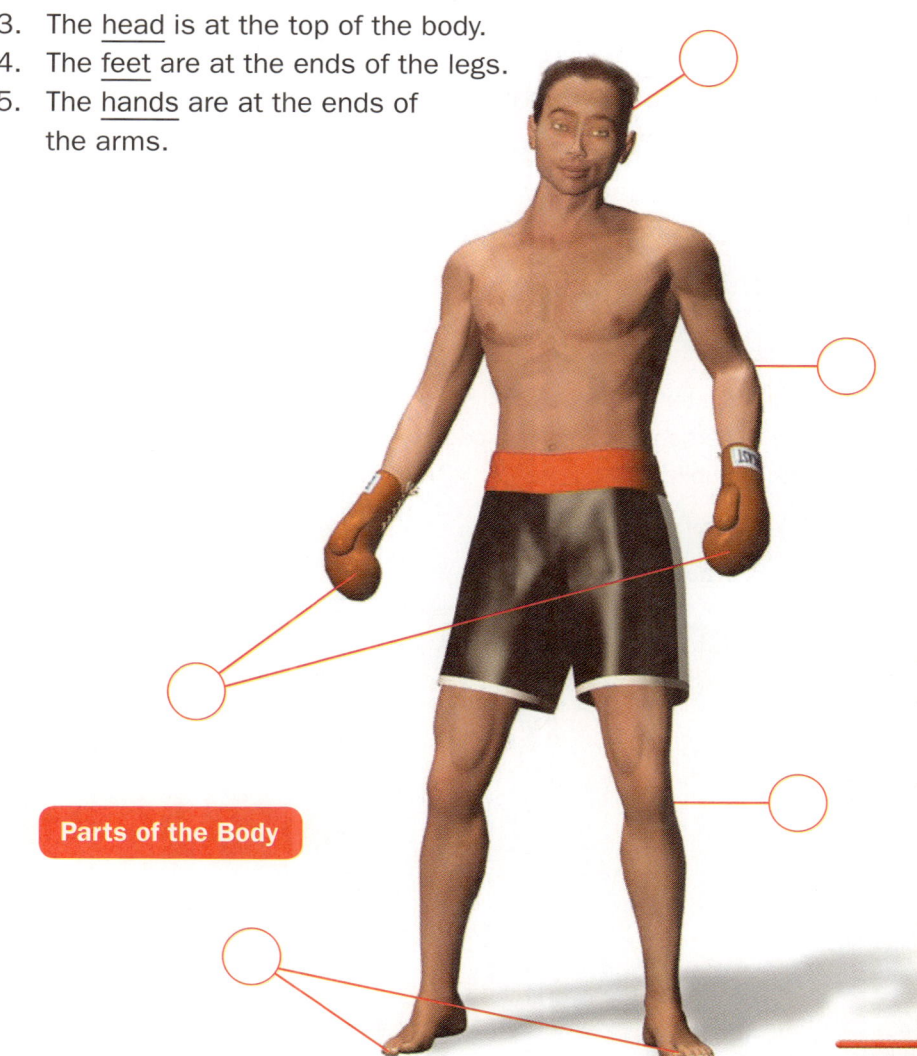

Parts of the Body

Thai boxing, or *Muay Thai*, is Thailand's most ancient martial art. It looks a little like Western boxing, but it's actually quite different. In Thai boxing you can use every part of your body: your hands, head, feet, knees—even elbows are allowed.

The sport has a long history. Two thousand years ago, **warriors**[1] trained in Thai boxing to protect their country from **invaders.**[2] Now, it's one of Thailand's most popular sports. Almost everyone in Thailand loves it. It's part of almost every **festival**[3] and it's shown on television around the whole country every day.

---

[1]**warrior:** a fighter
[2]**invader:** a person who enters a country or place by force
[3]**festival:** a public party

CD 3, Track 01

Two thousand years ago, Thai boxing started as a way to protect Thailand. Now, it's a popular sport.

Some of the most successful boxers in Thailand started boxing at the **Lanna Muay Thai Training Camp**[4] in Chiang Mai. Right now, the camp is home for a 12-year-old boy named Manat. He and 15 other boys have come here to become boxers.

Most of the boys are young and many come from poorer families. The camp pays for their training. While they are here, they do very little except box—all the time! The boys have to train for seven hours a day, seven days of the week. They train this hard with the hope of becoming the next great champion. For Manat and the others, success here could lead to better lives and a higher status in Thai society.

---

[4]**Lanna Muay Thai** [lɑnə mu̠aɪ taɪ] **Training Camp:** a place where Thai boxers live and practice

Fact Check: True or false?

1. You can't use your head in Thai boxing.
2. You can see Thai boxing on TV.
3. There are 15 boys at the training camp.
4. The boys come from families with a lot of money.
5. The boys train every day.

The camp was started by Canadian **coach**[5] Andy Thomson. Thomson explains why Thai boxing is so important for the boys: "Thai boxing offers the boys a chance at status … improve[d] status in their community, the opportunity to **earn**[6] some money, and most of them will have a dream of being a champion one day in **Lumphini Stadium**[7] in Bangkok. It's an opportunity to open up their world."

For Manat and the other boys, this is their big chance. It's a chance to see more than just their home village. It's also a chance to make their family and friends very proud.

---

[5]**coach:** person who leads, teaches, and trains people
[6]**earn:** make (money)
[7]**Lumphini Stadium:** [lumpini steɪdiəm] well-known large place in Bangkok for Thai boxing events

a coach

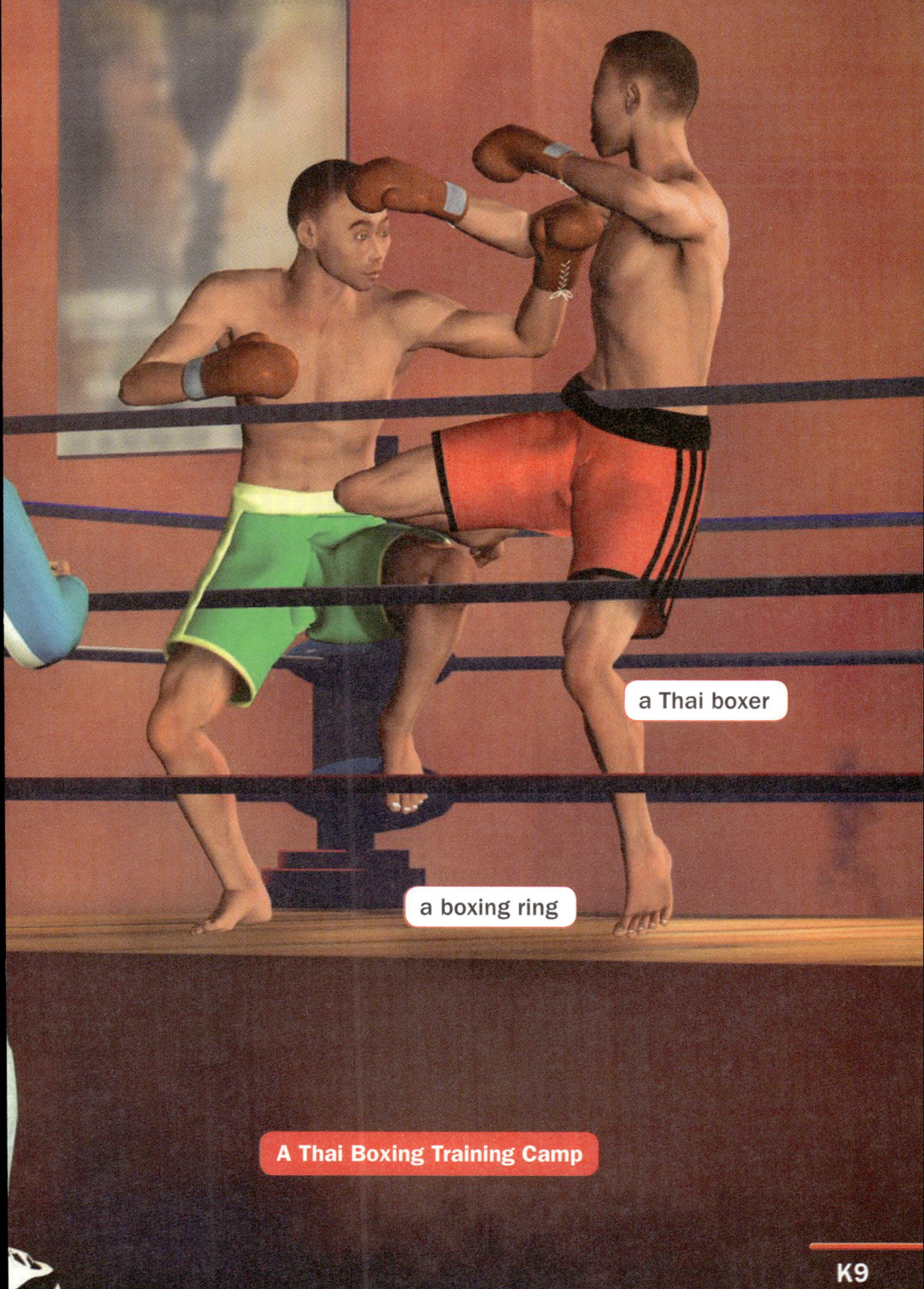

The boys may be dreaming of success, but right now they have a lot of work to do. Manat is getting ready for his second fight, which will happen tomorrow. He's been practicing a lot. Thai boxers have to be strong, but they also must practice very hard. It's not only about training their bodies. They also have to prepare their minds and the way they think about the fight.

Modern *Muay Thai* is about even more than just learning to think and fight like a warrior. It's also about achieving a personal goal. Helping his parents and making them proud is very important to Manat. He says: "If I move on to the bigger fights, one day I'll be a champion—a champion of Chiang Mai. I'll feel very proud and good. And I'll send the money I win to my parents."

A Thai Boxer prepares for his fight.

Manat's big night finally arrives. The fight is in a small town outside of Chiang Mai. Manat goes into the boxing ring for the '**Rama Muay.**'[8] This is an ancient ceremony which focuses a fighter's **strength**[9] and power. It helps him to get ready for the fight.

After the ceremony, Manat's important fight finally begins. But what are judges looking for in Manat's technique, or style of boxing?

---

[8]**Rama Muay:** [rɑmə muaɪ]
[9]**strength:** level of power

Coach Thomson explains: "The judges are looking for good, clean shot technique—both **offensive**[10] and **defensive**.[11] They are looking for the boxer who is in control of the fight," he says.

Manat fights hard, but for him tonight is not the night. He doesn't win the fight. What went wrong? Why didn't Manat win?

---

[10]**offensive:** moving forward against something to get an advantage
[11]**defensive:** protecting oneself from something

Scan for Information

Scan page K16 to find the information to answer the questions.

1. In the fight, what things do the judges look for?

2. How does Manat perform?

3. Does Manat win?

Thai Boxing Champion Manus Boonjumnong

Unfortunately, the boy Manat fought was taller, heavier, and more experienced than him. But even with these disadvantages, Manat did very well. He may have lost the fight, but his coaches now definitely believe in him. They believe that he can be a winner.

Thomson describes the fight: "Manat's fight was very good. He fought really well. [He had a] **good attitude** ... a **good heart**[12] ... very good heart." He then adds, "even though he's not happy, he'll be all right tomorrow. He'll be back fighting again— no problem."

Manat may not have won this fight, but it's okay. He must remember that tonight's fight was only one step in the long process of making a Thai boxing champion!

---

[12] **good attitude/good heart:** good way of thinking/strong will or mind

After You Read

1. What part of your body can you use in Thai boxing?
   A. elbows
   B. hands
   C. head
   D. all of the above

2. On page K4, 'protect' means:
   A. stop from
   B. take away
   C. keep safe
   D. join together

3. At the training camp, the boys box _____.
   A. daily
   B. sometimes
   C. rarely
   D. occasionally

4. Which is NOT a good heading for page K6?
   A. Champions Come from Chiang Mai Camp
   B. Boys Get a New Chance with Boxing
   C. Manat Is a Great Champion Boxer
   D. Training Is Not Easy for Boys

5. Andy Thomson believes that boxing in Thailand:
   A. is better than boxing in Canada
   B. gives boys a chance for a better life
   C. is an easy sport to be successful in
   D. can make everyone rich

6. Why does the writer say that Thai boxing is not only about training bodies?
   A. to explain that it's also about getting the mind ready
   B. to show that Manat must work harder than others
   C. to introduce Manat's third fight
   D. to show that most boxers are not prepared to fight

7. Modern *Muay Thai* is not _____ about learning to fight.
   A. at all
   B. really
   C. also
   D. just

8. According to page K12, what does Manat think is good about boxing?
   A. He can live away from home.
   B. He can learn about group goals.
   C. He can win every time.
   D. He can make his mother and father proud.

9. What is the ancient ceremony that Manat does in the ring?
   A. a fight of power and strength
   B. a way of preparing for the fight
   C. a meeting with the other boxer
   D. none of the above

10. In paragraph 1 on page K16, 'they' refers to:
   A. the boxers
   B. the coaches
   C. the judges
   D. Manat's family

11. What is a good heading for page K19?
   A. Manat Fought Well but Lost
   B. Manat Wins Big Fight
   C. Manat Is Happy after Fight
   D. Coach Worries about Boy

12. What does the writer think about Manat's future?
   A. He cannot be a champion.
   B. He is going to be a successful boxer.
   C. He will never be the champion of Chiang Mai.
   D. He will win the next fight.

Kano Jigoro, the Man Who Created Judo

by Julia Park

The country of Japan has a long history of martial arts that started over 2,500 years ago. Many different martial arts have developed since then. In these martial arts, fighters use their hands, feet, knees, elbows, and heads to fight. Ancient history says that Japanese warriors often used martial arts skills to protect their families and country. However, martial arts also had another purpose. They were used to train the mind. A good fighter had to be a skilled thinker.

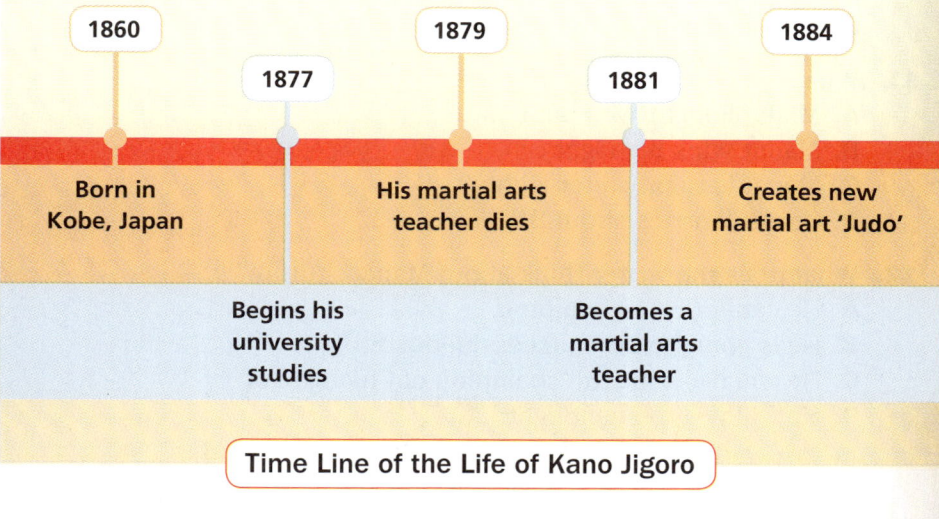

Time Line of the Life of Kano Jigoro

- 1860 — Born in Kobe, Japan
- 1877 — Begins his university studies
- 1879 — His martial arts teacher dies
- 1881 — Becomes a martial arts teacher
- 1884 — Creates new martial art 'Judo'

Judo involves thinking as well as fighting.

In the late 1800s, the best-known martial art was 'jujitsu.' However, jujitsu was about to experience an important change. A man called Kano Jigoro used his influence to develop a new form of jujitsu. He called this new form 'Judo.'

Kano Jigoro was born in Kobe, Japan, in 1860. When he was a small child, bigger boys would follow him and try to fight with him. One day, Jigoro learned a bit about jujitsu from a friend of his father. Jigoro was immediately interested. When he began his university studies, he also began the serious study of jujitsu. Two years later his teacher died. He had to find another teacher. By the time he was 21, Jigoro was very good at jujitsu and he had become a teacher himself.

As time passed, he began to develop a new type of martial art. It had many of the characteristics of jujitsu. However, Jigoro added some of his own ideas as well. He was especially interested in the thoughtful and spiritual side. He called this new form 'judo.' The word 'ju' means 'gentle' and 'do' means 'way.' Today millions of men, women, and children all over the world practice judo.

CD 3, Track 02

Word Count: 324
Time: _____

Vocabulary List

boxer (K: 2, 6, 9, 11, 14, 16)
boxing ring (K: 2, 9, 15)
ceremony (K: 2, 15)
champion (K: 2, 6, 8, 12, 19)
coach (K: 8, 19)
defensive (K: 16)
earn (K: 8)
elbow (K: 3, 4)
feet (K: 3, 4)
festival (K: 4)
good attitude/good heart (K: 19)
hand (K: 3, 4)
head (K: 3, 4, 7)
invader (K: 4)
knee (K: 3, 4)
martial art (K: 2, 4)
offensive (K: 16)
proud (K: 2, 8, 12)
status (K: 2, 6, 8)
strength (K: 15)
warrior (K: 4, 12)

Water Sports Adventure

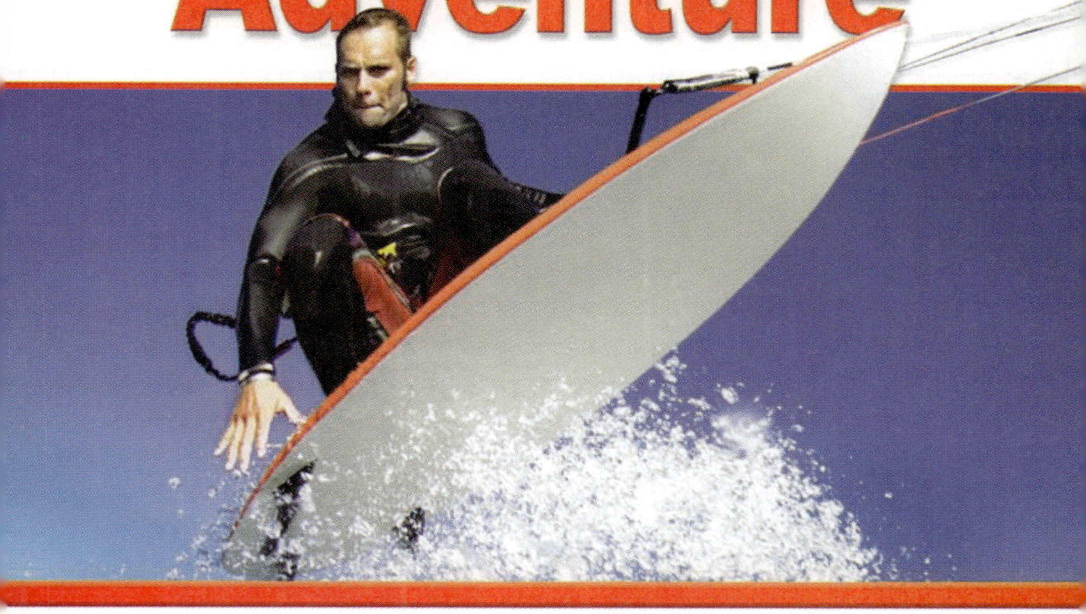

Rob Waring, *Series Editor*

Australia • Brazil • Japan • Korea • Mexico • Singapore • Spain • United Kingdom • United States

Words to Know

This story is set in the United States (U.S.). It happens in the Columbia River Gorge, in the states of Oregon and Washington.

A **Water Sports.** Read the paragraph. Then, write the number of the correct underlined word next to each item in the picture.

Water sports are usually very fast and fun! In water-skiing **(1)**, a person stands on one or two thin skis and a very fast boat **(2)** pulls the skiier over the water. In wakeboarding **(3)**, a person stands on a special wide board and a boat pulls them along the water. In kiteboarding **(4)**, a person stands on the same kind of board, but a large kite pulls them. All of these activities can be very enjoyable—especially if the waves **(5)** on the water are big!

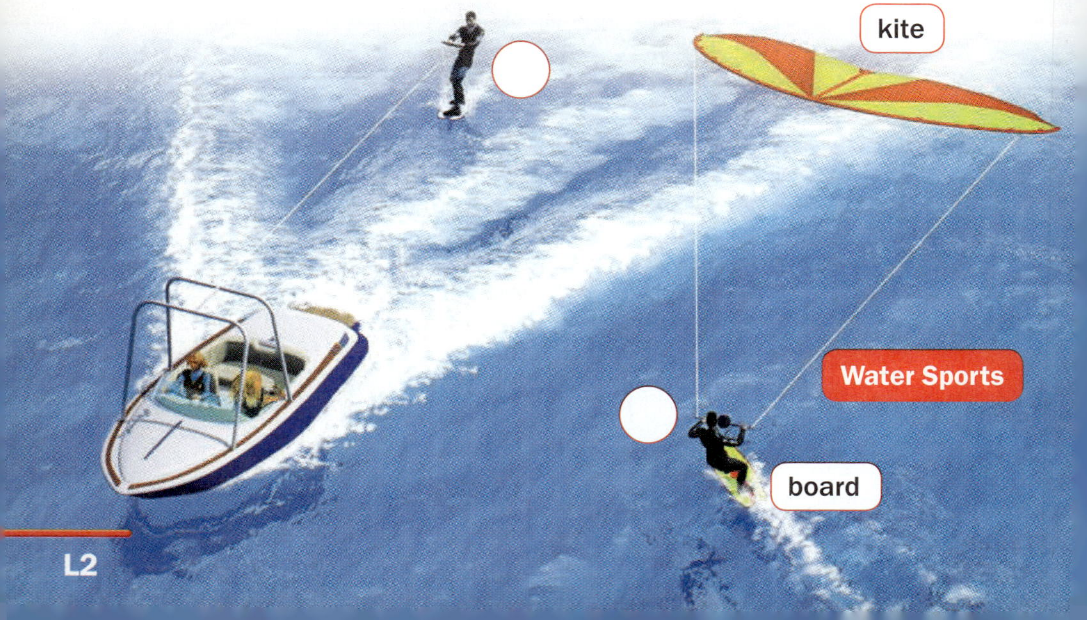

B **An Unusual Inventor.** Read the paragraph. Then, match each word with the correct definition.

This story is about water sports in the Columbia River Gorge. A gorge is an area between two mountains, so there is usually a lot of wind there. Cory Roeseler [reɪslər] lives in the area, and he loves new things and adventure! Roeseler is a mechanical engineer who likes to invent new things. He likes to design new sports equipment that uses the power of the wind.

1. gorge _____
2. wind _____
3. adventure _____
4. mechanical engineer _____
5. invent _____
6. design _____
7. equipment _____

a. a narrow place between two high areas
b. new and different experiences
c. a natural, fast movement of air
d. someone who studies how machines work
e. make or draw plans for something
f. things used for a particular activity or purpose
g. create something that has never been made before

skis

It's a cold winter day in the Columbia River Gorge. "[I] can't believe what blue sky we've got today! It's beautiful," says Cory Roeseler as he prepares his equipment. It may not be warm, but for Roeseler, the wind makes it a perfect day.

To most people, the very cold wind would feel uncomfortable. However, it gives Roeseler a different feeling. He says, "[It] feels like power … feel some wind!" He then adds, "It's going to be good today." But good for what? Roeseler puts on a special suit for water sports. He then starts to carry a big kite down to the water. "Okay, let's go **sailing**,"[1] he says with a smile.

---

[1] **sail:** move with the power of the wind, usually with a cloth called a 'sail'

 CD 3, Track 03

You see, Cory Roeseler doesn't just fly kites on windy winter days. Roeseler flies with them! Thirty-year-old Roeseler was one of the first people to really experience the sport of kiteboarding. He uses a kite to catch the power of the wind. This wind power has helped Roeseler to do new and interesting things. It's been especially helpful in developing new adventure sports, like kiteboarding.

But what is kiteboarding like? How does it feel? According to Roeseler, "It's sort of a **rolly**,[2] **wavy**,[3] free feeling … where you know at any moment, you can just **launch**[4] off the water for a few seconds and fly."

---

[2] **rolly:** *(slang)* move from side to side because of wind or waves
[3] **wavy:** *(slang)* move up and down because of wind or waves
[4] **launch:** go up into the air quickly

And that's exactly what Roeseler does! As the kite pulls him quickly along, he lifts himself out of the water and launches into the air. That may be why the young mechanical engineer compares kiteboarding to the way birds fly. He says that the power of the wind in a kite can be like a bird moving its **wings**.[5] The lifting power, or 'lift,' of both things can **overcome gravity**.[6] This lift allows them both to 'fly'.

---

[5]**wing:** part of a bird's body that is moved to fly
[6]**overcome gravity:** become stronger than the natural force that pulls things to Earth

The power of the wind in a kite is like the lift of a bird's wings.

Wind power is something that's easily found in the gorge which divides Washington and Oregon. That makes the Columbia River Gorge one of the best places in the world to kiteboard. However, for inventor Cory Roeseler, the gorge is more than just a place to have fun; it's a place where he can test his new inventions.

Roeseler has always loved water sports. When he was a teenager, he was the first person to 'test pilot,' or try out, the sport of kite-skiing. Usually, people water-ski behind a boat. However, Roeseler decided to use wind power to ski behind a kite. It worked! Later, he became a mechanical engineer. Then, in the 1990s, he invented and designed a lot of water sports equipment. Eventually, he became famous in the area of water sports.

Sequence the Events

What is the correct order of the events? Write numbers.

_____ invented water sports equipment

_____ became famous

_____ was a test pilot for kite-skiing

_____ became mechanical engineer

Now, Roeseler is ready to test his newest invention for playing with the wind. To do this, Roeseler has asked his friends for some help. He takes the group to the water to show them his invention. It's a new kind of wakeboarding boat that has a sail on the back. Roeseler explains how the sail works. "The sail's going to **stabilize**[7] us so we don't **tip over**,"[8] he says excitedly.

However, his friends don't seem as certain. Roeseler's friend Jeff, who will be testing the invention, is watching **nervously**[9] nearby. "Why are you nervous?" someone asks. "I've never seen anything else like that before," he says, laughing. "So it's a little **freaky**,"[10] he explains. But what makes Roeseler's boat so different?

---

[7] **stabilize:** keep in place; stop sudden changes
[8] **tip over:** fall to the side
[9] **nervous:** worried about a future event
[10] **freaky:** unusual in an unpleasant or unexpected way

In recent years, more and more people have started using towers for wakeboarding. A tower is a structure that is put on a wakeboarding boat. It allows people to place the wakeboarding rope higher. This higher rope gives more lift to the wakeboarder and makes it easier to jump in the air. It's also easier on the wakeboarder's body.

Roeseler's design is similar to that of other wakeboarding boats. However, his tower is 17 feet off the water. That's six feet higher than other wakeboarding boats. The higher rope will allow the wakeboarder to jump even higher than before! Roeseler has also added a sail to the tower. The sail will stabilize the tower and the wake boarder when the boat is moving.

1 foot = 0.31 meters

Jeff jumps into the water and the boat starts to move. As the boat goes faster, he is able to stand up on his wakeboard. He then starts moving quickly and easily across the water. After a few moments, he speeds up, goes towards a wave, and launches high into the air. The new invention works! Everyone is very happy. "Nice!" says Jeff as he gets back in the boat. "It works," he says with surprise. "It's **nuts**.[11] I didn't think it would!"

And how does Roeseler feel about the apparent success of his invention? "I'm a little more **confident**[12] … but, we'll see. It's got to go on a big wakeboard boat and get tested in the right environment," he explains.

---

[11]**nuts:** crazy or not normal; not expected
[12]**confident:** certain of one's abilities

For Cory Roeseler, the right environment seems to be the Columbia River Gorge. For him it's the right place to live, and the right place to find adventure with his new water sports.

According to Roeseler, life sometimes seems almost too good to be true. For him and his friends, living in the area is so wonderful that it's like being in a **dream**.[13] He adds that they're also happy that they're not going to wake up and find that it's gone. It seems like Roeseler and his friends want every day to be a water sports adventure!

---

[13]**dream:** events and images experienced in the mind while sleeping

Infer Meaning

1. How does Cory Roeseler feel about the Columbia River Gorge?
2. What does he mean by 'it's like being in a dream'?

After You Read

1. On page L4, how does Cory Roeseler feel about the wind?
   A. uncomfortable
   B. happy
   C. unsure
   D. nervous

2. In paragraph 1 on page L7, the word 'experience' means:
   A. fly
   B. use
   C. do
   D. be

3. How does the kite help Roeseler?
   A. It catches the wind and provides lift.
   B. He uses it to pull his boat.
   C. It keeps him warm.
   D. It reduces his speed.

4. Kiteboarding feels _____ flying.
   A. just
   B. about
   C. way
   D. like

5. Which is NOT a good heading for page L10?
   A. Inventor Tests Inventions in Gorge
   B. Kiteboarders Like Windy Area
   C. River Gorge Wind Too Strong
   D. Fun at River Gorge

6. When Roeseler started kite-skiing, he was:
   A. under ten years old
   B. 12 years old
   C. between 13 and 19 years old
   D. thirty years old

7. In paragraph 1 on page L12, 'it' refers to:
   A. a new invention
   B. the wind
   C. a kite
   D. a wakeboard

8. According to page L12, what do Roeseler's friends think about the new wakeboarding boat?
   A. They think it's great.
   B. They think it will work well.
   C. They are not sure about it.
   D. They really don't like it.

9. What's new about Roeseler's wakeboard boat?
   A. It has a tower.
   B. It has a rope.
   C. It's a smaller boat.
   D. It has a higher tower than other boats.

10. In paragraph 2 on page L14, the word 'allow' means:
    A. gives
    B. lets
    C. makes
    D. agrees

11. Roeseler thinks his latest invention:
    A. needs more testing
    B. is nuts
    C. is unbelievable
    D. works perfectly

12. Why can every day be a perfect day for Roeseler?
    A. He can kiteboard every day of the year.
    B. He loves where he lives and what he does.
    C. The weather is usually windy in the gorge.
    D. all of the above

My Water-Skiing Adventure

June 12

Well, this is it…. I'm taking my first water-skiing lesson tomorrow morning. I'm a little nervous, but it'll be an adventure!

June 13

I met my teacher early this morning. Before we started, he said I had to practice on dry land. First, he asked me to sit down on the ground. Then he gave me the 'tow rope,' the line that will connect me to the boat. While he held the rope, I had to stand up only using the power in my legs. It wasn't easy. I'm just not used to doing that! He also told me to remember one important thing—I must drop the tow rope immediately if I fall over.

Then the fun really began. We put the equipment into the boat and went out into deep water. My teacher said that he would start the boat slowly and then go faster. My job was to stand up when the boat was going quickly. It sounded easy. But as soon as I stood up, I tipped over. Then, I forgot to drop the rope! I went flying through the water and my skis came off. I felt really silly and we had to start again. I tried this twenty-five times, but I could not stand up. Water-skiing is harder than I expected.

Water-skiing is hard work but fun!

June 14

Today things were a little better. After five attempts, I was able to stand up. I waited until I found my balance on the skis, and then stood up slowly. I was surprised at how hard the water felt under the skis. It was like stone. The wind on my face was really strong. I was water-skiing and it felt wonderful!

June 15

Today was even better than yesterday! There were some big waves and I learned how to move over a wave without falling. Tomorrow I'm going to try it using only one ski—I can't wait!

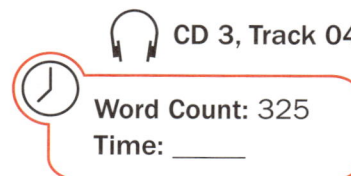

CD 3, Track 04

Word Count: 325
Time: _____

Vocabulary List

adventure (L: 3, 7, 18)
boat (L: 2, 10, 12, 14, 17)
confident (L: 17)
design (L: 3, 10, 14)
dream (L: 18, 19)
equipment (L: 3, 4, 10, 11)
freaky (L: 12)
gorge (L: 2, 3, 4, 10, 18, 19)
invent (L: 3, 10, 11, 12, 15, 17)
kiteboarding (L: 2, 7, 8, 10)
launch (L: 7, 8)
mechanical engineer (L: 3, 8, 10, 11)
nervous (L: 12)
nuts (L: 17)
overcome gravity (L: 8)
rolly (L: 7)
sail (L: 4, 12, 14)
stabilize (L: 12, 14)
tip over (L: 12)
wakeboarding (L: 2, 12, 14, 17)
water-skiing (L: 2, 10)
wave (L: 2, 17)
wavy (L: 7)
wind (L: 3, 4, 7, 8, 9, 10)
wing (L: 8, 9)

Dinosaur Search

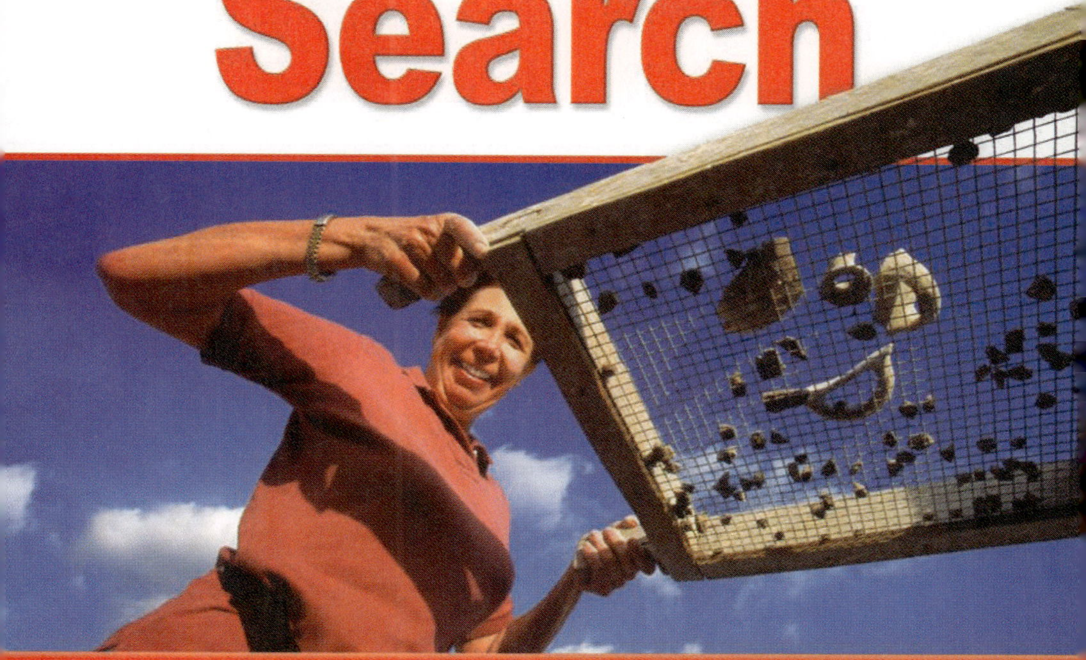

Rob Waring, *Series Editor*

HEINLE
CENGAGE Learning

Australia • Brazil • Japan • Korea • Mexico • Singapore • Spain • United Kingdom • United States

Words to Know

This story is set in Niger, which is a country in Africa. It happens in the Sahara [səhærə] Desert.

A **Parts of a Dinosaur.** Read the sentences. Write the number of the correct underlined word next to each item in the picture.

1. The shoulder girdle joins the body and the arms or front legs.
2. The pelvis joins the body and the back legs.
3. The limbs are the arms and legs of a body.
4. The jaw is the lower part of the face that moves when the mouth opens.

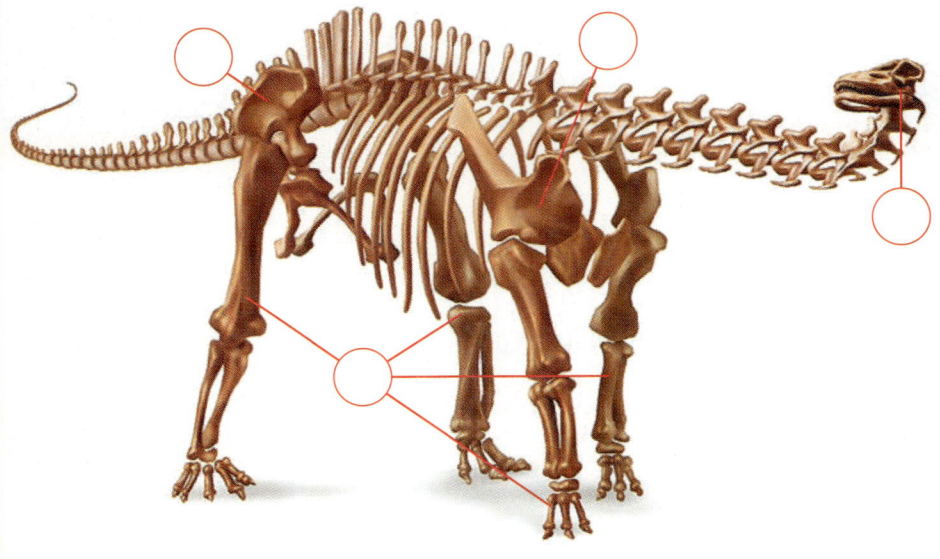

A Dinosaur Skeleton

B Fossils in the Desert.
Look at the pictures and read the paragraph. Then, complete the paragraph with the words in the box.

| bones | fossils | prehistoric |
| desert | paleontologists | sand |

Dinosaurs are (1)_____ animals. They lived long before people documented history. The scientists who study them are called (2)_____. These scientists often study dinosaur (3)_____, or the hard parts inside the body. They also study animal and plant parts that have been saved in rock. These are called (4)_____. In this story, a team of scientists looks for dinosaur parts in the (5)_____. The dry air there helps save the dinosaur bones. However, sometimes the (6)_____ covers up the bones so they are difficult to find.

Prehistoric Bones and Fossils

The Sahara Desert is also known as Africa's dinosaur **graveyard**.[1] The Sahara is one of the best places to look for the bones of prehistoric animals. It's a place that has many **secrets**.[2] Some of these secrets have been hidden under the sand for hundreds of millions of years. Now, a team of scientists is searching for these secrets.

---

[1]**graveyard:** an area of land where dead bodies are found under the ground
[2]**secret:** something no one knows about; something hidden

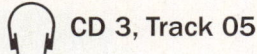 CD 3, Track 05

Paleontologist Dr. Paul Sereno and his team are in the Sahara looking for **clues**.[3] They hope that these clues will lead them to dinosaur bones. These bones may help them to better understand dinosaurs and the time period in which they lived. Dr. Sereno explains: "We're **on the trail of**[4] a number of dinosaurs. We begin to **paint a much better picture**[5] of this time [period] each time we come [to the Sahara]."

The team drives across the desert. Then suddenly, one of the team members says, "Hey! Back there!" The team stops to look around the area. They're near the right place!

---

[3] **clue:** a sign or information that helps to solve a problem or answer a question
[4] **on the trail of:** following; trying to find
[5] **paint a better picture (of something):** get a better understanding or image of something

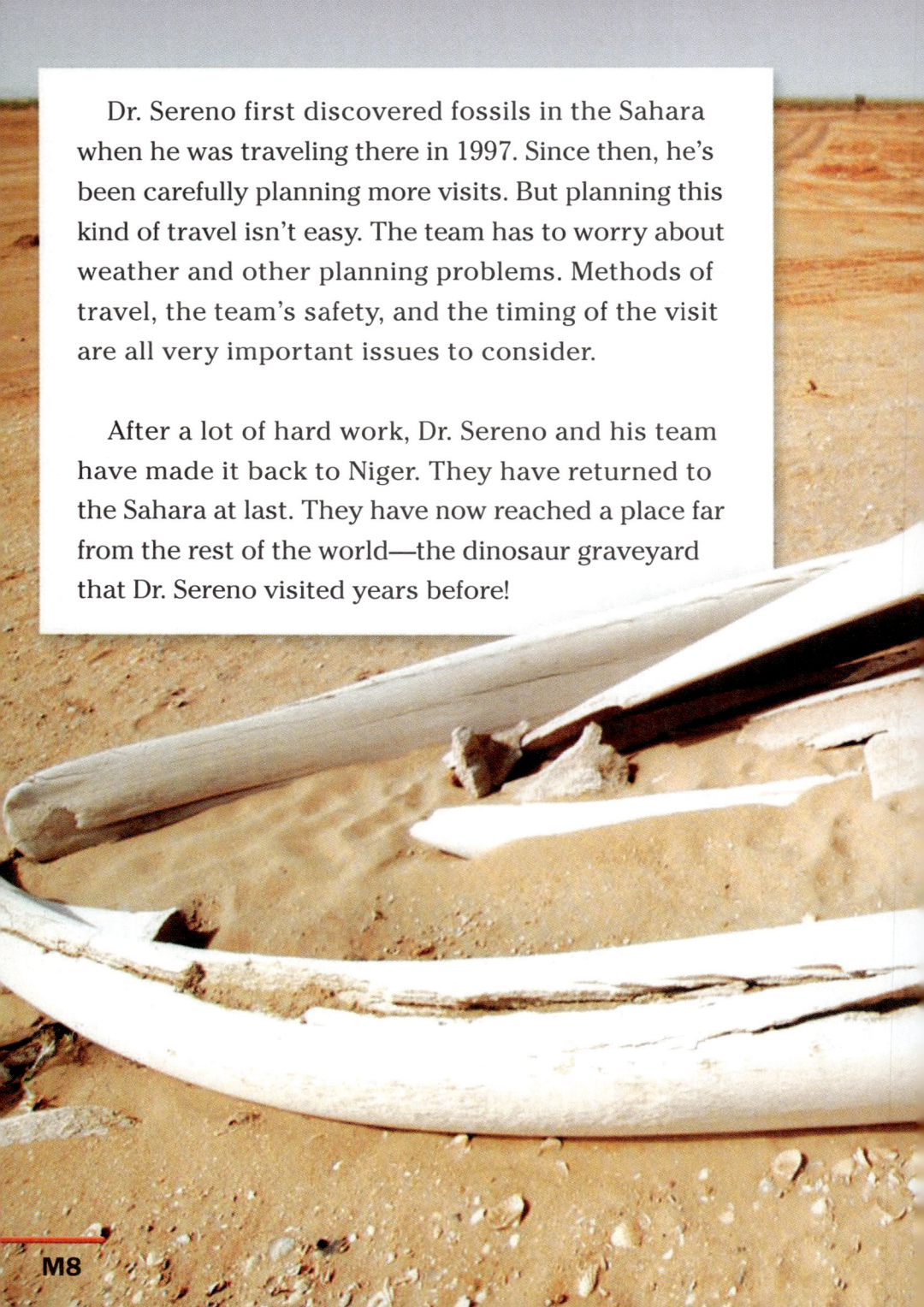

Dr. Sereno first discovered fossils in the Sahara when he was traveling there in 1997. Since then, he's been carefully planning more visits. But planning this kind of travel isn't easy. The team has to worry about weather and other planning problems. Methods of travel, the team's safety, and the timing of the visit are all very important issues to consider.

After a lot of hard work, Dr. Sereno and his team have made it back to Niger. They have returned to the Sahara at last. They have now reached a place far from the rest of the world—the dinosaur graveyard that Dr. Sereno visited years before!

Scan for Information

Scan page M8 to find the information.

1. When did Dr. Sereno first discover fossils in the Sahara Desert?

2. What problems do Dr. Sereno and his team have when visiting the Sahara Desert?

3. Where is the team now?

Now that the team is in the correct place, the dinosaur search can begin! There are bones everywhere in this dinosaur graveyard.

It doesn't take the team a long time to discover them. They talk about the bones as they find them. "It's part of a shoulder girdle," says one team member, as he picks up a bone. Another team member finds something else. "It's a **distal end**[6] of a limb bone right there," he says as he points to the end of a bone. And another: "We've got what looks like a leg."

Nearby, there's another discovery. "Hey look at this!" says one member. "It's a pelvis!" However, as another team member comes closer to see the bone, he gets in trouble. "Wait, you're stepping on it!" says the team member who found it. Everyone needs to be very careful with these prehistoric bones and fossils!

---

[6]**distal end:** part farthest away from where something is attached

The dinosaur search continues. The team finds bones from several prehistoric animals. They have collected a lot of **promising**[7] fossils, and are very happy about it. Unfortunately, life isn't so good for the team in other ways.

The desert is a hot place, and the team has used up most of their water. They are now worried because the water truck hasn't arrived yet. "After today, we'll have a day and a half's worth of water," says one team member. "We're just hoping for the water truck to get here in time," he adds. Luckily, it does!

Their water worries are over, and there's one more thing they don't have to worry about…

---

[7]**promising:** likely to be very good or helpful in the future

... and that's finding enough fossils! The team makes one important discovery after another. They carefully document each find.

Then, one day as they are walking around, they make their biggest discovery yet; they find the jaw of the prehistoric crocodile sometimes called 'super croc'! This discovery is big—very big—and the jaw bone is in very good condition.

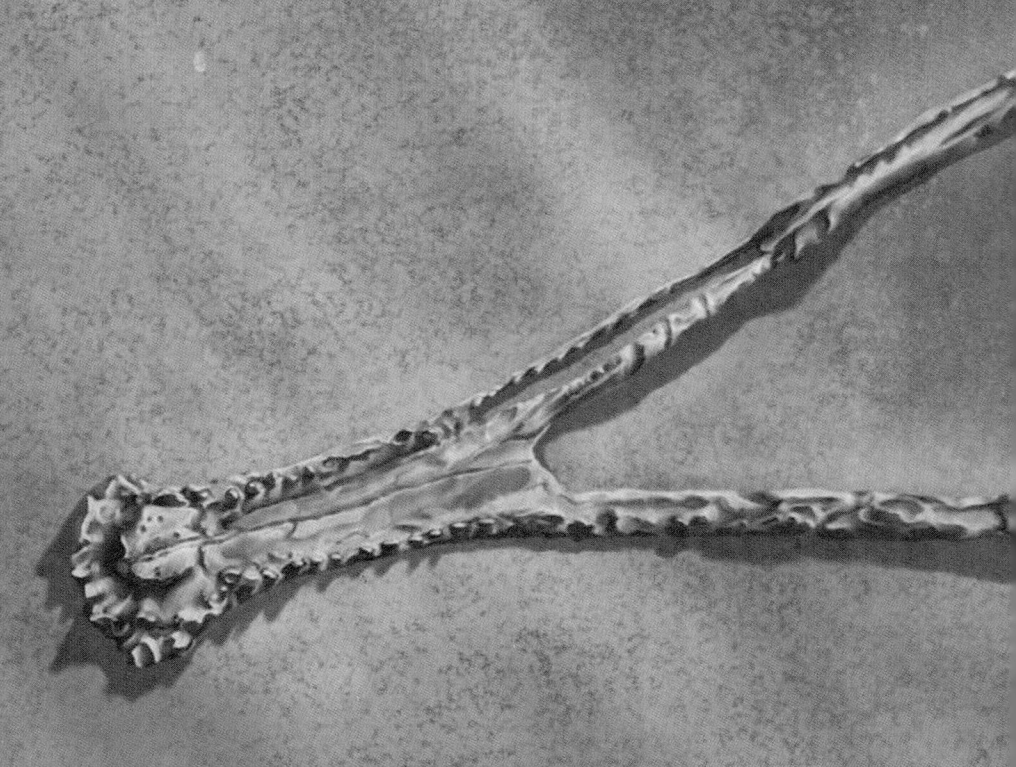

The paleontologists make a big discovery!

In fact, the discovery of the jaw bone is so important that the team soon gets a visit. National Geographic crocodile expert Brady Barr comes to the work site. Barr looks at the super croc bones with Dr. Sereno as they talk about the super croc. This ancient animal was very, very large. It was far bigger than the crocodiles that live today. The questions that scientists have about super croc are big too. What did it look like? What did it eat? How did it **hunt**?[8]

---

[8]**hunt:** catch and kill animals for food
*See page M24 for a metric conversion chart.

Brady Barr and Dr. Sereno can't answer these questions yet. However, they do realize that they probably won't find the answers in the desert sand. They will likely find them in the **swamp**.[9] Studying the crocodiles of today may tell these experts even more about the 110-million-year-old bones.

The paleontology team has made a great discovery on this dinosaur search. However, now that they have found these bones, a new search—one for more information—must now begin.

---

[9]**swamp:** area of very wet, soft land; crocodiles often live there

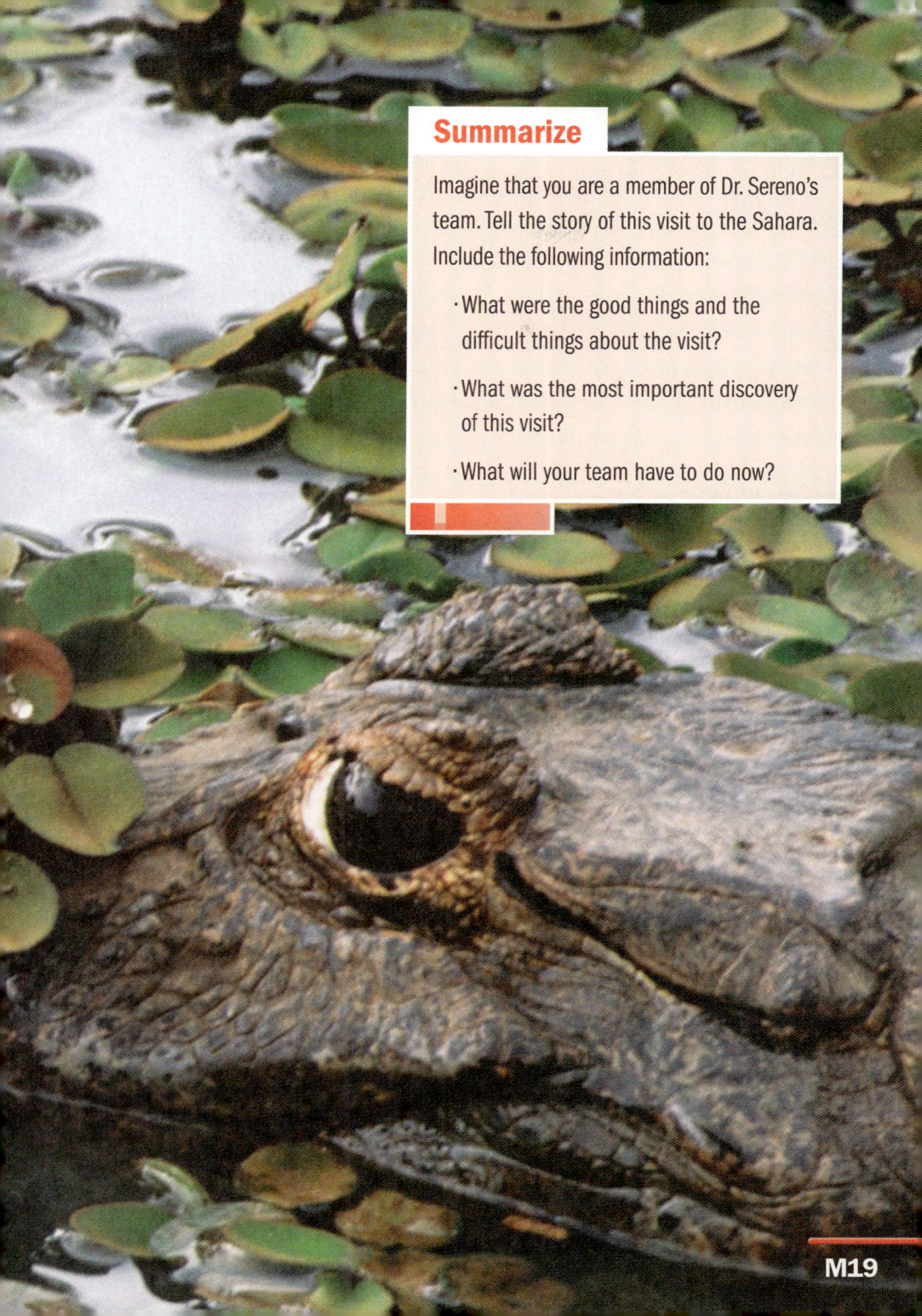

Summarize

Imagine that you are a member of Dr. Sereno's team. Tell the story of this visit to the Sahara. Include the following information:

- What were the good things and the difficult things about the visit?
- What was the most important discovery of this visit?
- What will your team have to do now?

After You Read

1. On page M4, the word 'team' can be replaced by:
   A. test
   B. researchers
   C. group
   D. class

2. In the Sahara Desert, secrets have been hidden _____ many years.
   A. during
   B. for
   C. in
   D. under

3. In paragraph 1 on page M7, 'them' in 'will lead them' refers to the:
   A. bones
   B. clues
   C. dinosaurs
   D. paleontologists

4. Dr. Sereno thinks the bones can teach us about:
   A. history
   B. the Sahara
   C. trails
   D. paleontologists

5. According to page M8, which of the following is NOT a problem in planning visits?
   A. safety
   B. weather
   C. timing
   D. fossils

6. What is a good heading for paragraph 2 on page M8?
   A. Team Arrives at Fossil Site
   B. Graveyard Close to Home
   C. Sereno Comes Often to Visit
   D. Team Leaves the Sahara

7. What's the main purpose of page M11?
   A. to show that the team is unsure about the bones
   B. to show that the team is never careful
   C. to show that there are many different kinds of fossils
   D. to teach us about different kinds of bones

8. The best heading for page M12 is:
   A. Promising Water Supply
   B. Not Enough Water
   C. Plenty of Bones, Plenty of Water
   D. Water Never Arrives

9. The team _____ uses all of their water.
   A. still
   B. almost
   C. never
   D. maybe

10. On page M14, 'document' means to:
   A. record
   B. analyze
   C. refer
   D. decide

11. What is significant about the super croc discovery?
   A. the importance of the discovery
   B. the size of the fossil
   C. the good condition of the fossil
   D. all of the above

12. Why is the answer in the swamp?
   A. because the sand is too deep
   B. because the swamp is very old
   C. because they must study living crocodiles
   D. because the rest of the bones are there

Dinosaur Discoveries

Dinosaur Eggs

Paleontologists know that dinosaurs grew and developed inside eggs. These eggs were hard and they protected the young dinosaurs. The process is similar to how birds grow and develop nowadays. However, dinosaur eggs are different from bird eggs. The outside of a dinosaur egg is much heavier. Dinosaur eggs are also a lot bigger than bird eggs. Dinosaurs created special places to keep their eggs safe and warm called 'nests'. Birds also build nests for their eggs. Most birds build their nests in trees. However, prehistoric dinosaurs built their nests on the ground. Interestingly, paleontologists think that dinosaurs covered their nests with dead plants to keep the eggs warm. A few of today's birds also do this.

Dinosaur Eggs

Dinosaur Footprints

Dinosaur footprints range in size—some are very small and some are very large. These footprints were made millions of years ago when the ground was soft and wet. Later on, sand filled the footprints. As time passed, this earth and sand turned into stone and the footprints remained in the stone. Nowadays, paleontologists can tell a lot from dinosaur footprints. For example, the depth of the footprint helps them to understand how heavy the dinosaur was. Recently, paleontologists have discovered lots of footprints going in the same direction. This means that dinosaurs probably traveled together in large groups.

Dinosaur Footprints

Dinosaur Fossils

The best dinosaur fossils were formed when three things happened in a very short period of time. First, the dinosaur died. After that, the soft parts of the dinosaur went into the earth. The dinosaur bones remained on the ground. Finally, the bones and dinosaur parts were covered by sand before any were lost or broken. Paleontologists study fossils to learn about dinosaurs. They are always searching for new fossils. However, it is not always easy to find them. Fossils are usually discovered in two ways. Sometimes the wind wears the earth away. This makes it easier for paleontologists to spot new fossils. Other times fossils are uncovered by workers preparing to build a new road or building.

CD 3, Track 06

Word Count: 335
Time: _____

Vocabulary List

bone (M: 3, 4, 7, 11, 12, 14, 17, 18)
clue (M: 7)
desert (M: 3, 4, 7, 9, 12, 18)
distal end (M: 11)
fossil (M: 3, 8, 9, 11, 12, 14)
graveyard (M: 4, 8, 11)
hunt (M: 17)
jaw (M: 2, 14, 17)
limb (M: 2, 11)
on the trail of (M: 7)
paint a better picture (of something) (M: 7)
paleontologist (M: 3, 7, 15, 18)
pelvis (M: 2, 11)
prehistoric (M: 3, 4, 11, 12, 14, 16)
promising (M: 12)
sand (M: 3, 4, 18)
secret (M: 4)
shoulder girdle (M: 2, 11)
swamp (M: 18)

Metric Conversion Chart

Area
1 hectare = 2.471 acres

Length
1 centimeter = .394 inches
1 meter = 1.094 yards
1 kilometer = .621 miles

Temperature
0° Celsius = 32° Fahrenheit

Volume
1 liter = 1.057 quarts

Weight
1 gram = .035 ounces
1 kilogram = 2.2 pounds

The Memory Man

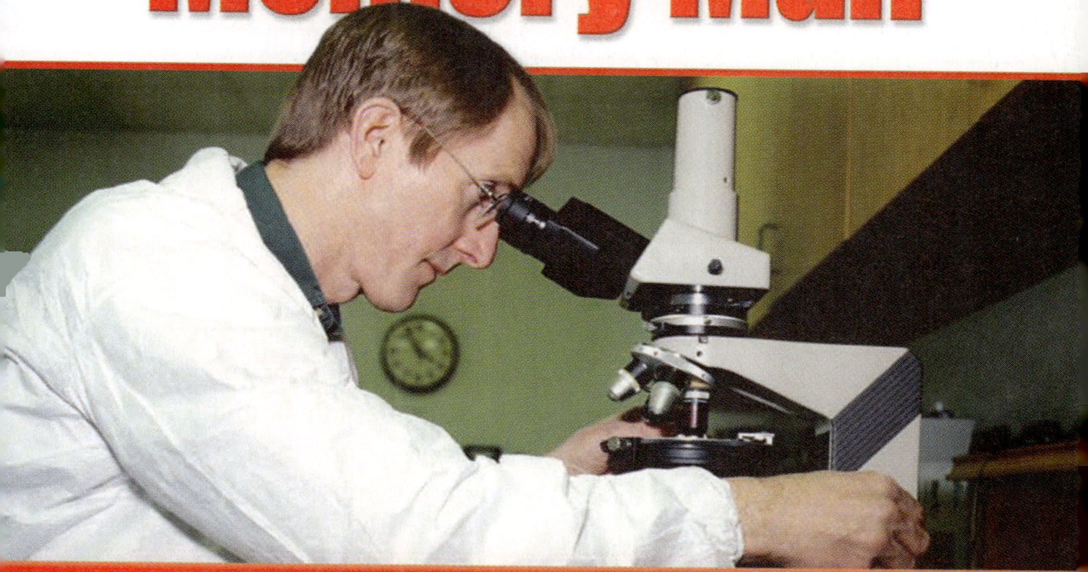

Rob Waring, *Series Editor*

Australia • Brazil • Japan • Korea • Mexico • Singapore • Spain • United Kingdom • United States

Words to Know

This story is set in Europe. It happens in the country of Italy.

A **Environment or Family?** Read the paragraph. Use the correct form of the underlined words to complete the sentences.

Gianni Golfera [dʒɑni gɔlfɛrə] has a very good <u>memory</u>. He can remember a lot of information. The <u>capacity</u> of his mind is so big that many scientists want to study it. Some think his good memory is because of his <u>environment</u>. They think his actions and the things around him improved his memory. Other scientists think that Gianni got his good memory from his parents' <u>genes</u>. They think memory characteristics come from the DNA of family members.

1. A _____ is a part of DNA that controls a certain characteristic.
2. _____ is the ability to remember.
3. The amount that something can contain is its _____.
4. Your _____ is the situation that you live in; what's around you.

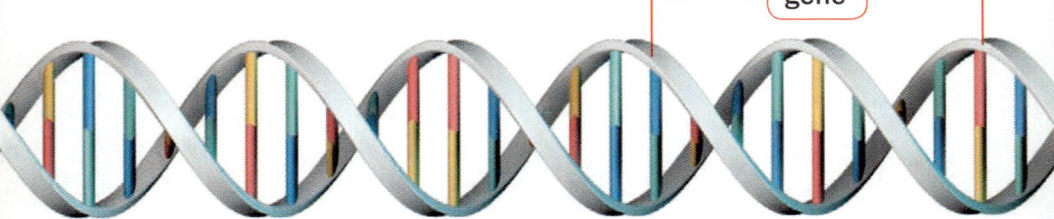

B **Memory and the Brain.** Look at the pictures and read the paragraph. Then match each word with the correct definition.

Dr. Malgaroli [mælgərouli] is a kind of scientist called a neurobiologist. He studies the human brain and the nerves connected to it. In this story, Dr. Malgaroli studies Gianni Golfera to find out why he has a good memory. He thinks the answer may be in a part of the brain called the hippocampus. Researchers have studied the hippocampus. They have found that it is important in adding information to our memories. In it, information is coded, or recorded, in the brain.

1. neurobiologist _____
2. brain _____
3. hippocampus _____
4. researcher _____
5. code _____

a. someone who studies a subject in detail
b. a scientist who studies the brain and the nervous system
c. change information so that it can be stored
d. part of the brain which has to do with memory
e. organ in the head that controls thought, feeling, and movement

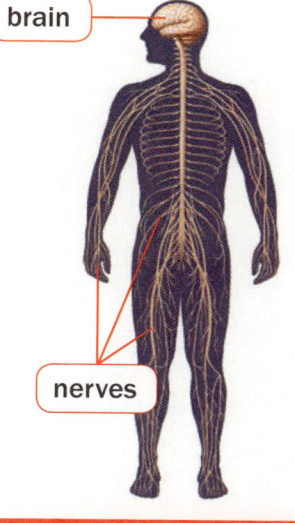

The Human Nervous System

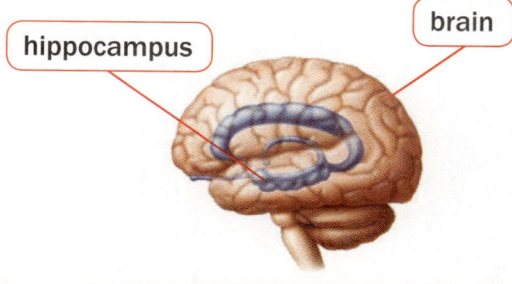

The Brain and the Hippocampus

Gianni Golfera is in front of a group of people. He's **blindfolded**,[1] but he can still show these people something that's amazing. The young Italian man calls it 'the art of memory.' First, the people who are watching him **randomly**[2] choose sixty numbers. After that, a helper reads the numbers to Gianni. Then, after hearing them just a single time, Gianni repeats the numbers in the correct order from memory. He does this first in the order he heard them. Then, he does it again—backwards!

---

[1] **blindfolded:** wearing something over the eyes so one cannot see
[2] **random:** done or chosen without any plan or system

 CD 3, Track 07

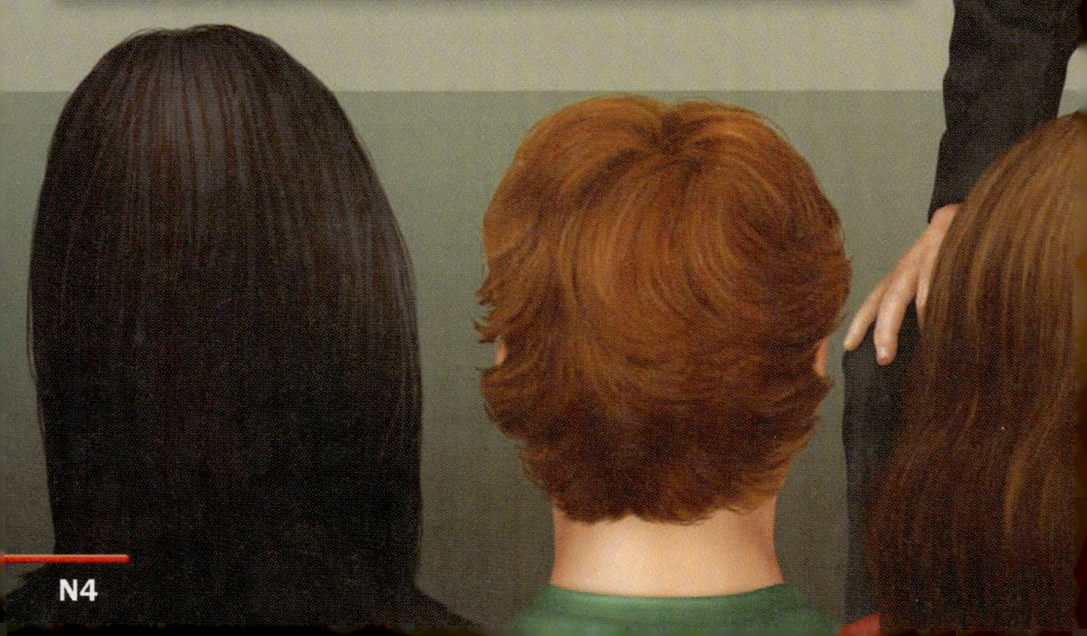

Gianni Golfera can remember long lists of numbers— forwards and backwards!

Gianni has a very special kind of memory. He explains in his own words: "It's a kind of memory that is connected to what I see. It means that every idea I learn, everything I read, becomes a part of me. Normally, a person who doesn't have this gift, and who hasn't studied memory, tends to just forget things—even an entire book. Not me." Gianni says that with his 'gift,' or special ability, he has **memorized**[3] more than 250 books!

Memorizing over 250 books is surprising, but it's not the only surprising thing about Gianni. He says that he can remember every detail of every day of his life. He also says that he can remember these details from the time he was less than one year old!

---

[3]**memorize:** learn something so that one can remember it exactly

Memory is very difficult to understand. Scientists don't really know how it works, yet. The Golfera family genes may hold important information about Gianni's memory. Neurobiologist Dr. Antonio Malgaroli plans to compare the Golfera family's genes with the genes of more forgetful families.

"The **crucial**[4] question," says Dr. Malgaroli, "is to understand which is the contribution from **heredity**,[5] and which is the contribution that comes from the environment."

---

[4]**crucial:** very important
[5]**heredity:** the passing of genes from parent to child

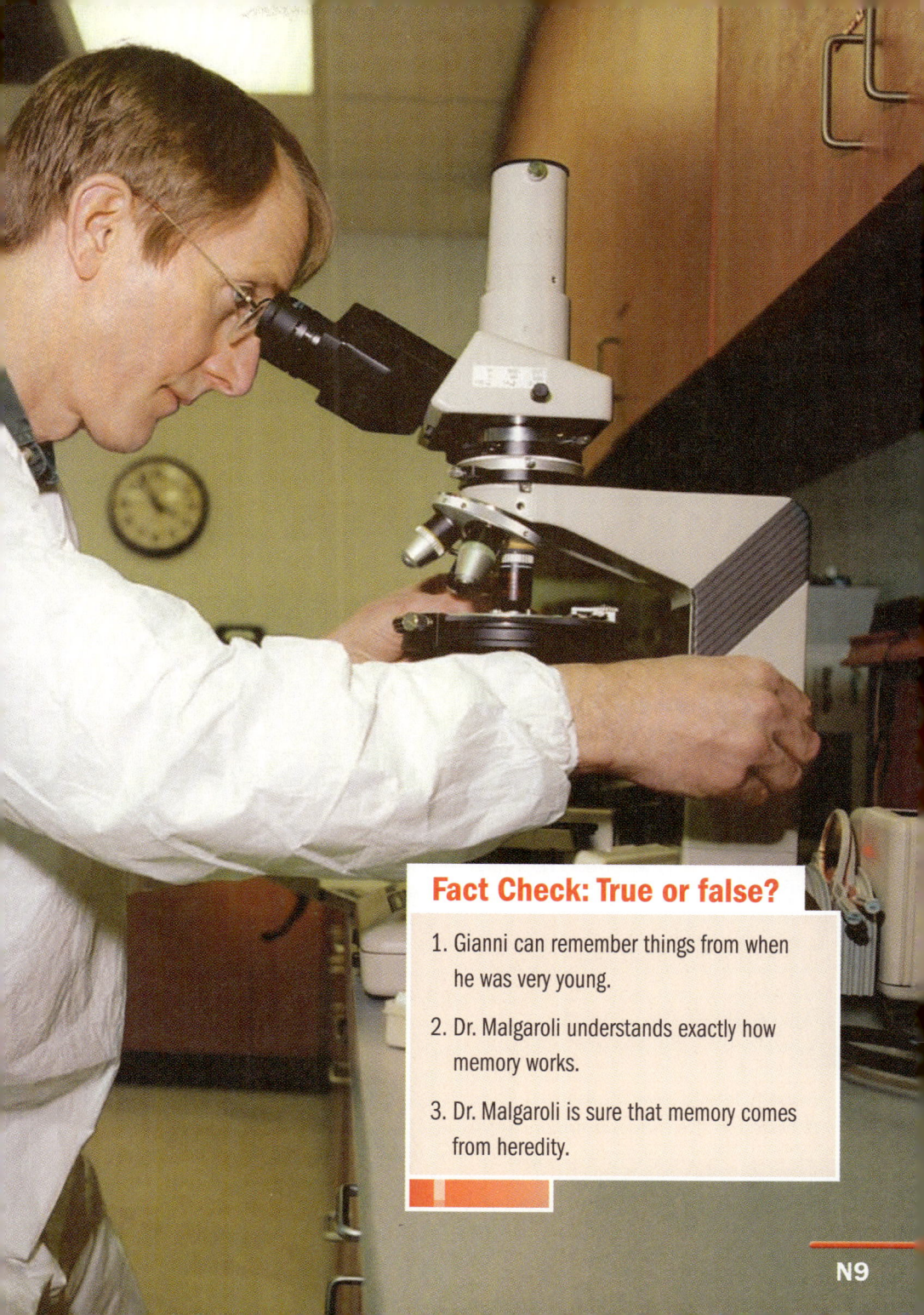

Fact Check: True or false?

1. Gianni can remember things from when he was very young.

2. Dr. Malgaroli understands exactly how memory works.

3. Dr. Malgaroli is sure that memory comes from heredity.

When we process new information, such as reading a book or newspaper, it goes into our brains. It gets into the brain through the part called the hippocampus. There, it's coded as memory. However, the actual process is still mostly unknown. How is memory coded? Where is it stored? Why is it stored there? These are all questions that are still unanswered. Nobody knows why or how these things happen. Nobody knows why some people lose their memories. They also don't know why so very few people are like Gianni and never forget things.

book

Nobody knows how memory is coded in the hippocampus.

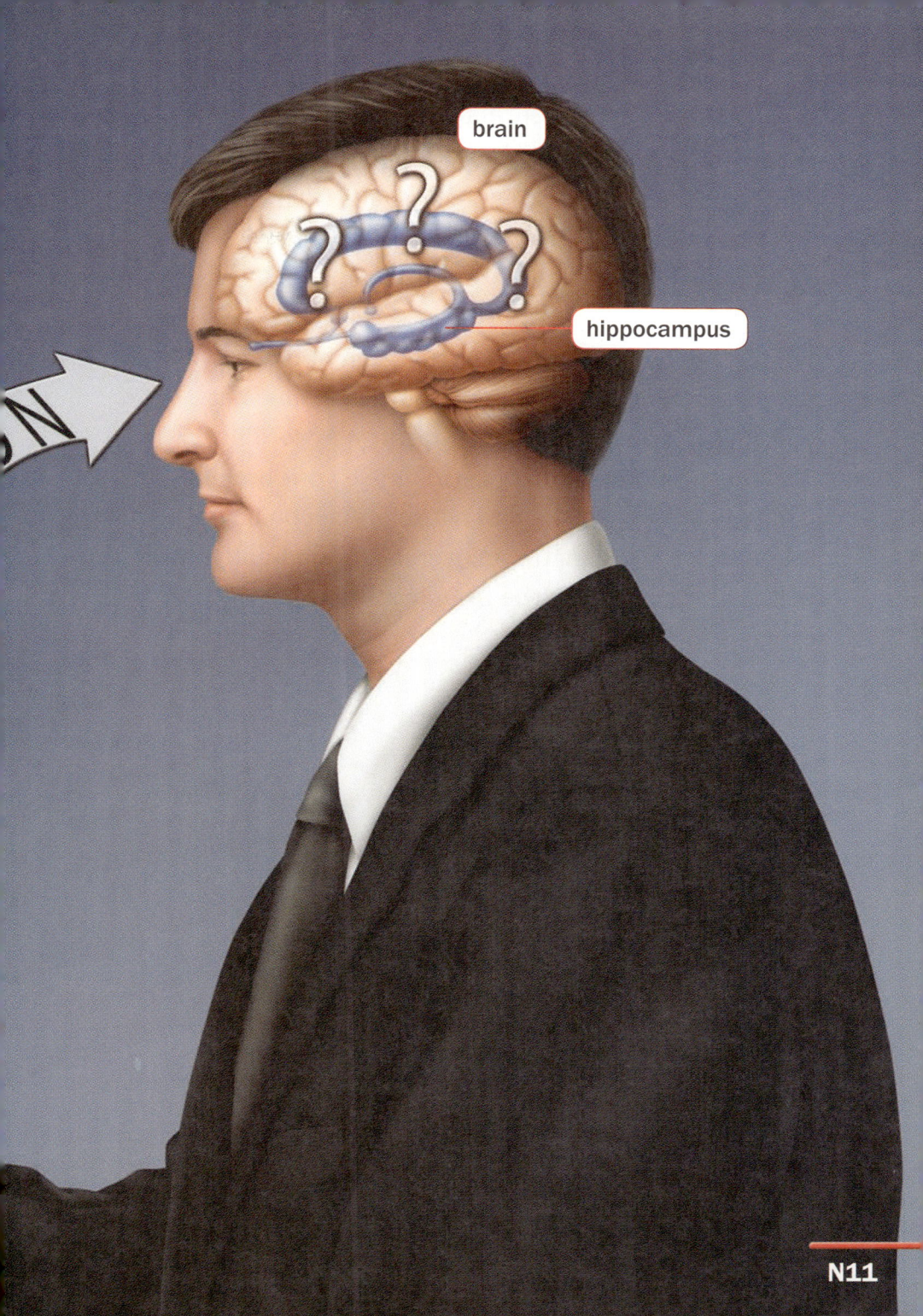

Researchers are now studying how memory and learning change the brain. They are also trying to match those changes to specific genes. They want to find out which memory characteristics are related to genes.

Some research already shows that a great memory may not depend on the right DNA only. It seems that everyone can remember more if they try. According to Dr. Malgaroli, "If you really need to use your brain capacity to store some kind of information, you have this ability. It's just a matter of exercise." Apparently, practice and exercising the brain can improve the memory!

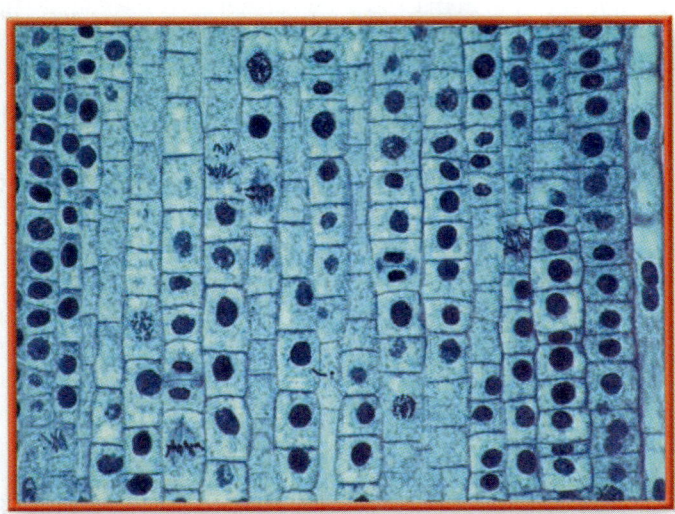

Identify the Main Idea

1. What is the main idea of Dr. Malgaroli's comment on page N12?

2. How does he think we can all improve our memories?

The same idea is true for Gianni. His genes are only part of the story. Since the age of 11, he's been training his brain to remember more and more. He practices continuously to improve the power of his memory. Gianni thinks about memory, and works on it, all the time. He has even memorized a whole series of historical books!

For Gianni, improving his memory has become almost like a full-time job. Dr. Malgaroli comments, "Golfera has an **extraordinary**[6] ability. The question is…how much it's really because of the Golfera family genes, and how much comes from his sort of '**maniac**'[7] type of activity."

---

[6]**extraordinary:** very special, unusual, or strange
[7]**maniac:** *(unusual use)* a person who spends most of their time on an activity of heavy interest

Gianni's life is not all about science, though. He has a relatively normal life. He has a dog and a girlfriend. He likes to take time away from work. In other words, he's just like other people, and that's part of what's so interesting about him. Gianni's genes may be partly responsible for his great memory. However, researchers think Gianni's memory is mainly because of his very hard work. Gianni agrees. He believes that anyone can do what he does.

Gianni even offers proof that anyone can have a great memory. He holds classes to teach others how to improve their memories. His system basically involves organization and hard work. In his classes, Gianni shows people how to organize their memories and how to 'remember to remember.' Gianni explains: "I think the only problem with memory is the correct order. There's a lot of brain space, so I think there are no limits."

If there is a memory gene, Gianni Golfera probably has it. But the success of 'The Memory Man' may be more about **determination**[8] than DNA. Gianni's practice and hard work are making his very good memory even better. At the same time, he might just be showing scientists that a great memory can be made and not just born!

---

[8]**determination:** continuing to try to do something, although it's very difficult

After You Read

1. What is Gianni doing in the classroom on page N4?
   A. learning about memory
   B. showing his ability to remember
   C. choosing sixty numbers
   D. helping read the numbers

2. On page N4, 'them' refers to:
   A. people
   B. Italians
   C. helpers
   D. numbers

3. What is NOT a good heading for page N7?
   A. Gianni Isn't Connected to World
   B. Man Never Forgets
   C. Young Italian Has Gift
   D. Memory Man Is Special

4. In paragraph 1 on page N7, Gianni _____ that every idea becomes a part of him.
   A. proves
   B. demonstrates
   C. says
   D. agrees

5. In paragraph 1 on page N8, the phrase 'more forgetful families' means:
   A. families who can't remember as well as Golfera's
   B. more families in general
   C. families who can't forget things
   D. families who have good memory genes

6. On page N8, where does Dr. Malgaroli think good memory comes from?
   A. family
   B. environment
   C. heredity
   D. He doesn't know.

7. On page N10, 'it' in 'it's coded' is referring to:
   A. memory
   B. new information
   C. old information
   D. brain

8. Exercising our brains can help us to remember _____.
   A. less
   B. much
   C. more
   D. often

9. Which of the following does Gianni NOT do to train his memory?
   A. He works a full-time job.
   B. He practices a lot.
   C. He thinks about memory.
   D. He memorizes books.

10. On page N17, the word 'relatively' means:
   A. strangely
   B. fairly
   C. totally
   D. oddly

11. Which of the following describes Gianni?
   A. He only reads about memory.
   B. He loves his job.
   C. He is a great scientist.
   D. He tries to lead a regular life.

12. What does the writer probably think about having a great memory like Gianni?
   A. Anyone can do it with a little work.
   B. Italian people have a special gene.
   C. Heredity and practice both help memory.
   D. Memory is determined by family.

How to Improve Your Memory

We still have a lot to learn about how memory works, but scientists do agree on certain ideas. Neurobiologists know that we store information in three memory systems in our brains. They also know that we process this information in three different ways. The following charts explain these systems and processes.

Process	Definition	How It's Done
Encoding	putting information into memory storage	• the brain notices and remembers what something means, how it sounds, or how it looks
Storage	keeping information in memory storage	• information is looked at again and again • similar ideas are grouped together
Retrieval	getting information from memory storage	• an existing thought is used to find an old idea that is stored in the brain

Information Processes of the Brain

Memory Systems of the Brain

Memory System	Information Source	Time Stored
Sensory Memory	the senses: eyes, ears, etc.	*12 to 30 seconds*
Short-Term Memory	sensory memory storage	*several minutes or hours*
Long-Term Memory	short-term memory storage	*many years*

Now that you understand how the brain works, here are three simple suggestions from brain researchers to improve your memory:

1. CHOOSE CAREFULLY

Don't try to remember everything. Decide what it is that you really need to remember. Then spend your time studying this key information. Don't let yourself think about unimportant information and ideas, even if you find them really interesting.

2. TRY SOMETHING NEW

The brain learns more when we keep it active. It gets stronger when it is given something new and unusual to learn. If you are a swimmer, learn how to play soccer. If you speak English, learn how to speak Spanish. Learning a new language is a great way to keep your brain active.

3. GET ENOUGH SLEEP

The brain needs sleep and rest. While you are sleeping, the brain organizes all the information that it processed during the day. If you don't get enough sleep, the information is not correctly stored. It is then difficult to remember things the next day, especially if you are very tired.

CD 3, Track 08

Word Count: 332
Time: _____

Vocabulary List

blindfolded (N: 4)
brain (N: 3, 10, 11, 12, 14, 18)
capacity (N: 2, 12)
code (N: 3, 10)
crucial (N: 8)
determination (N: 18)
environment (N: 2, 8)
extraordinary (N: 14)
gene (N: 2, 8, 12, 14, 17, 18)
heredity (N: 8, 9)
hippocampus (N: 3, 10, 11)
maniac (N: 14)
memorize (N: 7, 14)
memory (N: 2, 3, 4, 7, 8, 9, 10, 12, 13, 14, 17, 18)
neurobiologist (N: 3, 8)
random (N: 4)
researcher (N: 3, 12, 17)

Wild Animal TRACKERS

Rob Waring, *Series Editor*

HEINLE
CENGAGE Learning

Australia • Brazil • Japan • Korea • Mexico • Singapore • Spain • United Kingdom • United States

Words to Know

This story is set in South Africa. It happens in the Karoo [kəru] National Park. A **national park** is a special area where nature is protected.

(A) Wild Animals in Africa. Read the sentences and label the pictures with the underlined words.

A <u>herd</u> is a large group of animals.
Africa has many wild animals like <u>elephants</u>, <u>zebras</u>, and <u>giraffes</u>.
People often find wild <u>animal tracks</u>, or footprints, in Africa.

1. _____
2. _____ 
3. _____ 
4. _____ 
5. _____ 

02

B Conservation Technology.
Read the paragraph and notice the underlined words. Then answer the questions.

African Bushmen can track, or follow, animals very well. They can learn many things by tracking animals. However, the Bushmen can't always tell other people what they know. They don't always speak the same language. This story is about a conservationist named Louis Liebenberg (libənbɜrg). He is helping to protect Africa's wild animals. He has developed a new kind of technology for getting information about the animals. It's a method that doesn't depend on spoken language. It's called 'The Cyber Tracker.'

1. What does **'language'** mean? _____
2. What does **'conservationist'** mean? _____
3. What does **'technology'** mean? _____

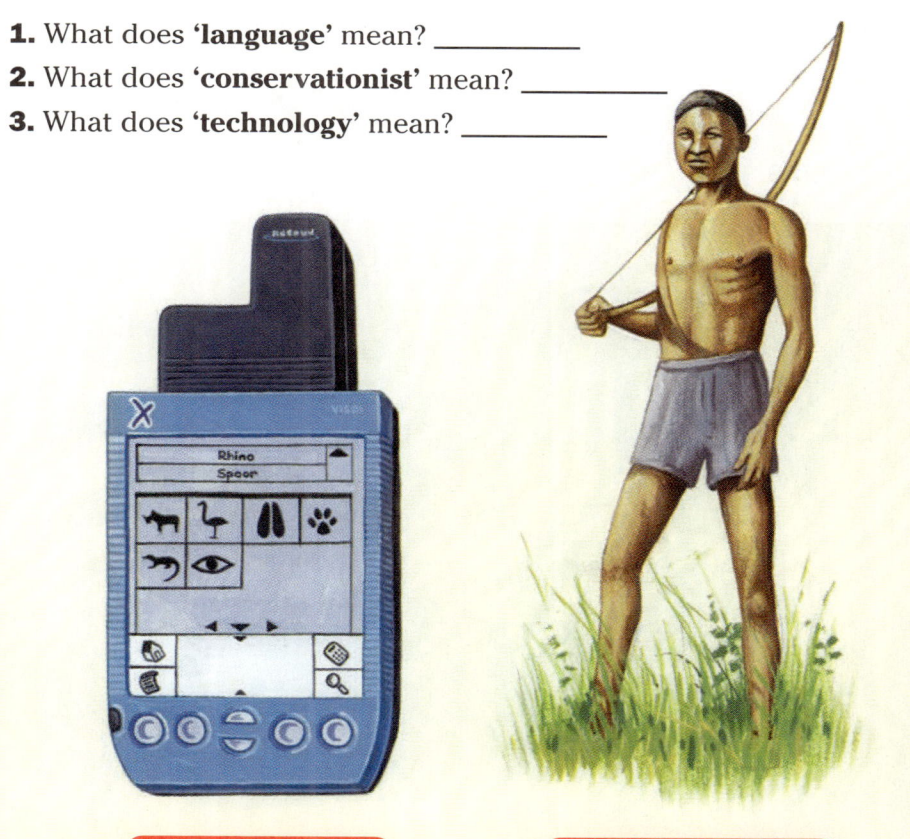

The Cyber Tracker   An African Bushman

In some parts of Africa, there are still big herds of wild animals like zebras, elephants, and giraffes. But today many of these wild animals are in danger because people are taking the land that the animals need.

It's a big problem that worries many conservationists. Conservationists are people who protect wildlife and nature. And some of these people are now leading a fight to save these animals.

CD 3, Track 09

Louis Liebenberg is one of the conservationists who is trying to save the wildlife of Africa. He feels that having good information about the animals is very important for success. "The most important thing is to try and get an understanding of what's happening out there," he says.

Liebenberg reports that people need to know more about animals. He says that people need to understand what happens to plants and animals over time. Are they increasing or decreasing in numbers? What plants are the animals eating?

Summarize

What does Liebenberg mean?

1. Summarize paragraph 1 in one sentence.
2. Summarize paragraph 2 in one sentence.

African Bushmen may be able to help conservationists to answer these questions. For hundreds of years, Bushmen have understood the ways of animals like zebras and giraffes. They're very good wild animal trackers. The Bushmen know what the animals eat. They know where the animals go. They even know where they sleep.

However, there is a problem. The Bushmen don't always speak the same language as the conservationists. This can cause problems when they work together, and communicating information is sometimes difficult. This is where new ideas and new technology can help.

This is where the Cyber Tracker comes in. The Cyber Tracker is an **invention**[1] created by Louis Liebenberg. Liebenberg has brought the invention to the Karoo National Park in South Africa. He hopes that together, the Cyber Tracker and the Bushmen can help protect the animals. He thinks it's a perfect match of modern technology and old knowledge. But what is the Cyber Tracker?

Liebenberg explains that it's a small computer that helps collect information about animals. It uses pictures, called 'icons,' instead of words to record information. This way, the Bushmen can record what they see even without words. They don't have to read or speak the same language as Liebenberg or others. According to Liebenberg, the Cyber Tracker can collect very detailed and **complicated**[2] information very quickly.

---

[1] **invention:** a new machine that has never been made before
[2] **complicated:** difficult; with many parts

However, that's not the only thing the Cyber Tracker can do. The small computer also contains a **global positioning device**.[3] Each time a Bushman sees something interesting about an animal or plant, he pushes a **button**.[4] The Cyber Tracker records exactly where the man is in the world. That way, even if the man can't read or write, he can record what he sees and where. But how does the Cyber Tracker record information?

---

[3] **global positioning device (GPD):** a machine that tracks where things are on Earth
[4] **button:** a small key on a machine

button

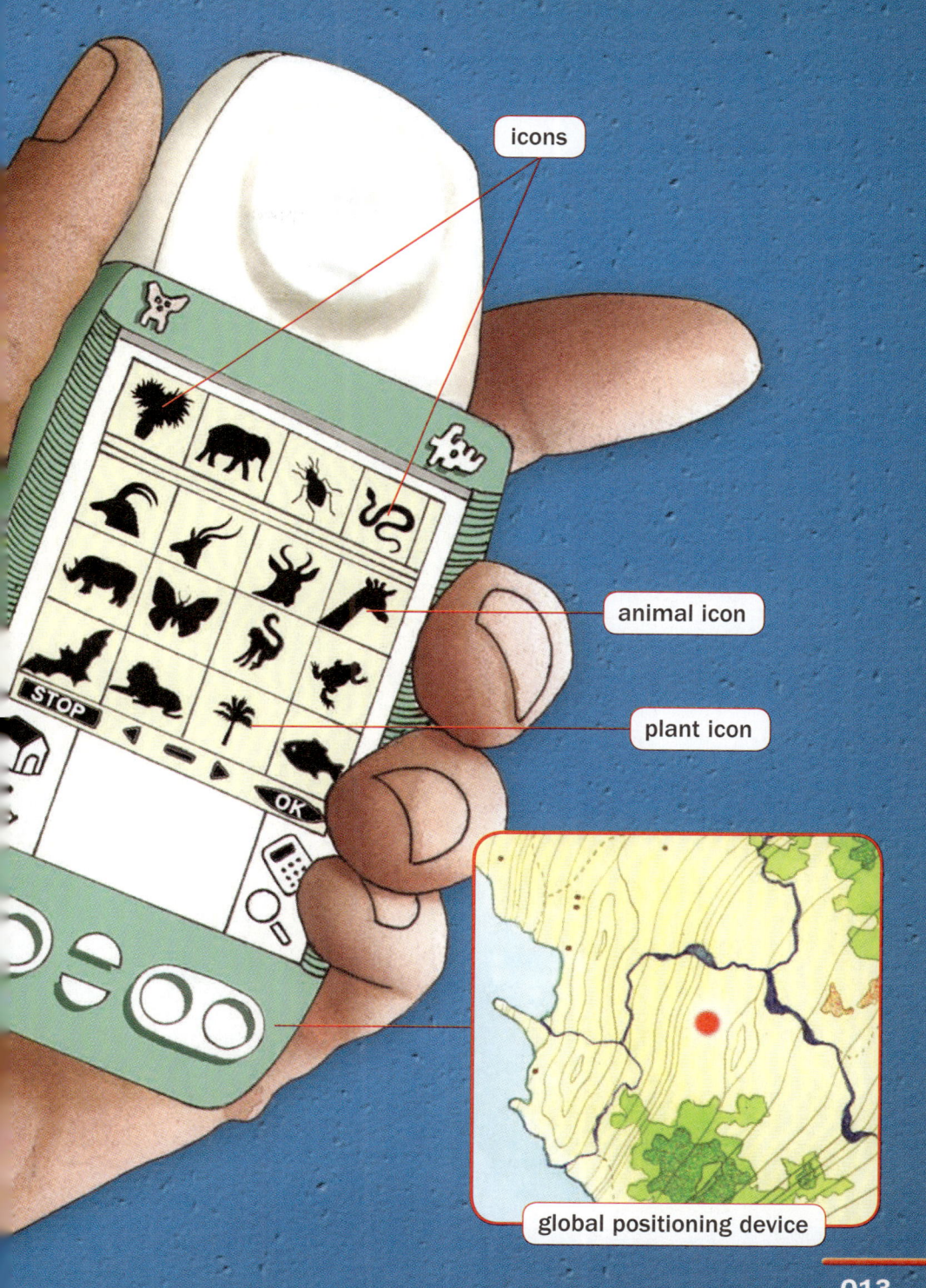

Liebenberg explains that the Cyber Tracker uses icons to communicate. There are pictures for drinking, walking, fighting, sleeping, eating, and other things. With the Cyber Tracker, the user can report whether an animal is sick or dead, too. The Bushman also can record other meanings by pushing different buttons. With this option, they can name about 50 different plants. This becomes very useful when the Bushmen want to record what the animals are eating.

However, Liebenberg adds that it's not just about the technology. According to him, the human factor is also very important. Liebenberg says that a big part of using the Cyber Tracker is the Bushman's ability to record the information. He must be able to understand and correctly report everything he sees. The combination of machine and man seems to work very well.

When the trackers return to their base, they connect the Cyber Tracker to a personal computer. Then, Liebenberg looks at the data and uses it to make **maps**.[5] These maps show where the animal herds are. They also give information about what the animals are eating, and indicate facts about their health. Liebenberg can get a lot of detailed information about a lot of wild animals.

---

[5]**map:** a detailed picture of a specific area

The Cyber Tracker project started five years ago. At first, the idea was to help a few animals in danger. Because of this, the invention was used only in certain situations. Nowadays, the Cyber Tracker is used much more often. More and more people have started using the Cyber Tracker in other African parks. They have also started using it with many different kinds of animals.

Recently, Liebenberg has even put the Cyber Tracker **software**[6] on the Internet. Now many conservationists around the world can get the software. They have started adding the technology to their conservation programs. The future of the Cyber Tracker looks good. Soon, it may be able to help in the conservation of wild animals everywhere.

---

[6]**software:** computer program

Scan for Information

Scan page 018 to find the information.

1. When did the Cyber Tracker project start?
2. What was it first used for?
3. Where can people get the software now?
4. What may the Cyber Tracker soon be able to do?

After You Read

1. Each of the following is happening to the animals in Africa EXCEPT:
   A. Conservationists are helping them.
   B. The land they need is being taken.
   C. There are fewer and fewer of them.
   D. They are in danger from the Cyber Tracker.

2. In paragraph 2 on page O4, the phrase 'leading a fight' is closest in meaning to:
   A. working hard
   B. arguing
   C. disagreeing
   D. protecting

3. The best heading for page O7 is:
   A. Animals Eat Plants and Increase
   B. Conservationist Wants to Know More
   C. Liebenberg Wants to Know Exact Number
   D. Conservationist Takes Space from Animals

4. Bushmen know _____ about animals.
   A. very
   B. nothing
   C. a lot
   D. too

5. In paragraph 1 on page O8, who is 'they' in 'they sleep'?
   A. animals
   B. bushmen
   C. conservationists
   D. Liebenberg's group

6. How does the Cyber Tracker make communication easy?
   A. People can see where the Bushmen are.
   B. The invention uses pictures for language.
   C. The software can identify about 50 plants.
   D. Conservationists can write down information.

7. The purpose of the Cyber Tracker is to:
   A. help with communication
   B. collect information about animals
   C. track animals
   D. all of the above

8. What initials are used for 'global positioning device'?
   A. GPS
   B. GPD
   C. GSP
   D. GDD

9. In the first sentence in paragraph 2 on page O15, 'it' refers to:
   A. technology
   B. global positioning device
   C. recording information
   D. pushing buttons

10. The Cyber Tracker helps to get _____ about animals and plants.
   A. maps
   B. computers
   C. information
   D. trackers

11. The writer probably thinks that:
   A. Every student should have the Cyber Tracker.
   B. Technology is making conservation easier.
   C. Louis Liebenberg is a famous software maker.
   D. The Cyber Tracker is difficult for conservationists.

12. According to page O18, which of the following will NOT happen in the future?
   A. The Cyber Tracker will be added to other conservation programs.
   B. The Cyber Tracker will be able to help animals everywhere.
   C. Conservationists won't be able to get the Cyber Tracker software.
   D. All of the above.

DAILY News

GLOBAL POSITIONING DEVICES BECOME INCREASINGLY COMMON

The invention of the satellite over fifty years ago opened the way for the Global Positioning System (GPS). GPS uses a series of satellites to provide exact information about the location, or position, of certain objects. There are currently 24 GPS satellites in use. There are also three additional satellites if one of the 24 stops working. Originally, only the United States government was able to use the system. Today, however, people everywhere can use GPS technology for free. This is making Global Positioning Devices (GPDs) much more common.

GPS uses a series of satellites.

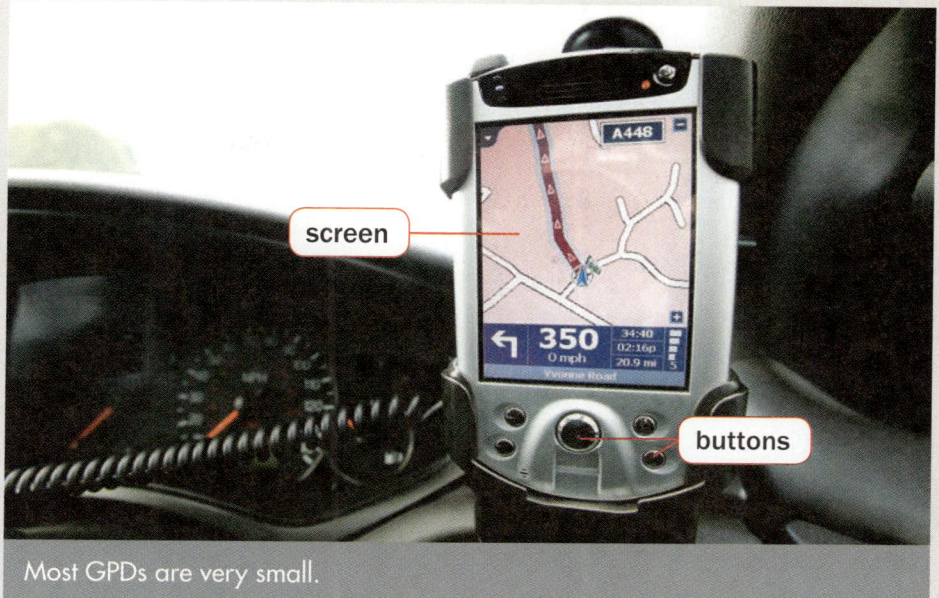

Most GPDs are very small.

A GPD is usually a small machine with a screen and several buttons on the front. They are often about the size of a cell phone. First, a GPD sends information to several satellites. This information tells the system where the user is; however, it must reach at least three satellites to work correctly. Next, GPS measures the GPD's exact distance from each satellite. It then sends this information back to the GPD. Finally, the GPD uses special software to change this information into a map with marks on it.

GPDs are like having a map that follows you wherever you go. They allow the user to see where he or she is at any moment. People can use the information to track where they have been or to plan where they want to go. Fishermen have discovered how useful GPDs can be when they are out on the open water. People lost in the woods can now find their way home. Many of today's new cars include GPDs. Drivers choose an end point and the GPD shows them the best way to get there. Some people are even placing GPDs on other people. They want to know where the person is at all times. The possible applications for GPDs are endless. Who knows where they'll show up next?

CD 3, Track 10

Word Count: 330
Time: _____

Vocabulary List

animal track (O: 2)
button (O: 12, 13, 15)
complicated (O: 11)
conservationist (O: 3, 4, 7, 8, 9, 18)
elephant (O: 2, 4)
giraffe (O: 2, 4, 8)
global positioning device (GPD) (O: 12, 13)
herd (O: 2, 4, 16)
invention (O: 11, 18)
language (O: 3, 8, 11)
map (O: 16)
software (O: 18, 19)
technology (O: 3, 8, 11, 15, 18)
zebra (O: 2, 4, 8)

Credits

Farley the Red Panda

Photography Credits:

TP © Joel Satore/National Geographic Image Collection, A6 © Ian Waldie/Getty Images, A7 © ZSSD/SuperStock, A8-9 © Ian Waldie/Getty Images, A10-11 © AFP/Getty Images, A12 © Adam Jones/Photo Researchers, Inc., A12-13 © Taylor S. Kennedy/Getty Images, A14 © AFP/Getty Images, A15 © imagebroker/Alamy, A18-19 © Duncan Usher/Alamy, A22 © Diez, O./Peter Arnold, Inc., A23 © Purestock/Alamy

Illustration Credits:

A2 (t) © Mapping Specialists, ltd. Madison, WI, USA, A2-3, A4-5, A20-21 © Jim Effler/American Artists Rep., Inc.

Gorilla Watching Tours

Photography Credits:

TP © Gerry Ellis/Getty Images, B4-5 © Nick Greaves/Alamy, B6 © Cat Gwynn/Getty Images, B7 © Ty Milford/Getty Images, B8-9 © Daryl Balfour/Getty Images, B10-11 © Roy Toft/Getty Images, B14 © Alissa Everett/Alamy, B14-15 © Gerry Ellis/Getty Images, B18 © Michael Nichols/Getty Images, B18-19 © Paul Souders/Getty Images, B22 © Jim Zuckerman/Corbis.

Illustration Credits:

B2 (t), B23 (t) © Mapping Specialists, Ltd. Madison, WI, USA, B2-3, B12-13, B16-17 © Alan Male/American Artists Rep., Inc.

Puffin Rescue!

Photography Credits:

TP © Frans Lemmens/Getty Images, C4-5 © Sisse Brimberg/Cotton Coulson/Keenpress/Getty Images, C6-7 © Richard T. Nowitz/CORBIS, C8 © Wolfgang Kaehler/CORBIS, C8-9 © Robert Patton/National Geographic Image Collection, C10-11 © Catherine Karrow/CORBIS, C14 © Johnathan Blair/CORBI5, C14-15 © Nordic Photos/Alamy, C18 © Richard T.Nowitz/CORBIS, C18-19 © Chris Gomersall/Alamy, C22 © J Marshall-Tribaleye Images/Alamy, C23 © AFP/Getty Images.

Illustration Credits:

C2 (t) © Mapping 5pecialists, Ltd. Madison, WI. USA, C2-3, © Gerard Taylor, iliustrationOnLine.com, C12-13, C16-17 © Mark Gerber.

A Disappearing World

Photography Credits:

TP © Robert Caputo/Getty Images, D4-5 © Kevin Schafer/Alamy, D6-7 © Gallo Images/CORBI5, D8 © Michael Nichols/Getty Images, D8-9 © Steve Bloom Images/Alamy, D12 © Patricio Robles Gil/Oxford Scientific Images, D12-13, D14-15, D18-19 © Michael Nichols/National Geographic Image Collection, D22 (t) © PhotoDisc/CD-Nature, Wildlife and Environment.

Illustration Credits:

D2 (t), D22 (b) © Mapping Specialists, Ltd. Madison, WI, USA, D2-3, D10-11, D16-17 © Mike Jaroska/American Artists Reps., Inc.

Credits (continued)

The Knife Markets of Sanaa

Photography Credits:
TP © Wolfgang Kaehler/CORBIS, E4-5 © TH Foto/Alamy, E8 © Tibor Bognar/Alamy, E9 © Egmont Strigl/Alamy, E10 © Danita Delimont/Alamy, E11 © Alex Ekins/Alamy, E14-15, © Wolfgang Kaehler/CORBIS, E16-17 © Stock Connection Blue/Alamy, E18-19 © Chris Mellor/Alamy, E22-23 (t) © PhotoDisc/CD-Nature, Wildlife and Environment, E23 © Anders Blomqvist/Getty Images.

Illustration Credits:
E2 (t), E22 (b) © Mapping Specialists, Ltd. Madison, WI, USA, E2-3, E6-7, E12-13 © Phil Saunders/American Artists Rep., Inc.

A Special Kind of Neighborhood

Photography Credits:
TP © David Sanger Photography/Alamy, F6 © Charles O. Cecil/Alamy, F8 © Dbimages/Alamy, F8-9 © Cicinelli, Elisa/Index Stock Imagery/Jupiterimages, F10-11 © AFP/Getty Images, F11 © Mark Richards/Photo Edit, F12-13 © Ty Milford/Getty Images, F14-15 © imagebroker/Alamy, F15 © Solveig Stibbe/Alamy, F18-19 © Robert Holmes/Alamy, F22 (t) © photoDisc/CD-Backgrounds and Textures, F23 © david mackenzie/Alamy.

Illustration Credits:
F2 (t), F22 (b) © Mapping Specialists, Ltd. Madison, WI, USA, F2-3, F4-5, F16-17 © Mike Jaroska/American Artists Reps., Inc.

The Last of the Cheju Divers

Photography Credits:
TP © David White/Alamy, G6-7 © AFP/Getty Images, G7 © AFP/Getty Images, G8 © JTB Photo/Photolibrary, G8-9 © JTB Photo/Photolibrary, G10-11 © AFP/Getty Images, G12 © Catherine Karnow/CORBIS, G12-13 © Wolfgang Kaehler/CORBIS, G14-15 © JTB Photo/Photolibrary, G15 © David White/Alamy, G18-19 © Pat Behnke/Alamy, G20-21 (t) © PhotoDisc/CD- Series-Color 1, G23 © David Fleetham/Alamy.

Illustration Credits:
G2 (t), G22 (b) © Mapping Specialists, Ltd. Madison, WI, USA, G2-3, G4-5, G16-17 © Phil Saunders/American Artists Rep., Inc.

Peruvian Weavers

Photography Credits:
TP © Danita Delimont/Alamy, H6-7 © Mark A. Johnson/CORBIS, H7 © willrolls.com/Alamy, H8-9 © Emmanuel LATTES/Alamy, H12-13 © mediacolor's/Alamy, H13 © Steve Vidler/Photolibrary, H14 © Gail Mooney-Kelly/Alamy, H15 © David Norton Photography/Alamy, H16 © David Norton Photography/Alamy, H17 © Gail Mooney-Kelly/Alamy, H18-19 © Arco Images/Alamy, H22-23 © Image Source/Corbis, H22 © Geoffrey Kidd/Alamy

Illustration Credits:
H2 (t)© Mapping Specialists, Ltd. Madison, WI, USA, H2-3, H4-5, H10-11 © Phil Saunders/American Artists Rep., Inc.

Taiko Master

Photography Credits:

TP © Mark Downey/Getty Images, I6-7 © Gary Conner/Photo Edit, I10-11 © Brent Winebrenner/Lonely Planet Images, I12 © 2007 Getty Images, I12-13 © Christian Kober/Photolibrary, I14-15 © James Quine/Alamy, I15 © Robert M. Vera/Alamy, I16-17 © Gary Crabbe/Alamy, I18-19 © Rich Iwasaki/Alamy, I22-23 (t) © PhotoDisc/CD-Background Textures, I23 © Jed Share/Getty Images.

Illustration Credits:

I2 (t), I22 © Mapping Specialists, Ltd. Madison, WI, USA, I2-3, I4-5, I8-9 © Phil Saunders/American Artists Rep., Inc.

Cheese-Rolling Races

Photography Credits:

TP © Cotswolds Photo Library/Alamy, J6-7 © Cotswolds Photo Library/Alamy, J8 © Cotswolds Photo Library/Alamy, J8-9 © Cotswolds Photo Library/Alamy, J12 © Cotswolds Photo Library/Alamy, J12-13 © Cotswolds Photo Library/Alamy, J14-15 © Cotswolds Photo Library/Alamy, J15 © Cotswolds Photo Library/Alamy, J16-17 © Cotswolds Photo Library/Alamy, J18 © Cotswolds Photo Library/Alamy, J18-19 © Cotswolds Photo Library/Alamy, J22-23 © eStock Photo/Alamy, J22 © Jeff Greenberg/Alamy.

Illustration Credits:

J2 (t) © Mapping Specialists, Ltd. Madison, WI, USA, J2-3, J4-5, J10-11 © Garad Taylor/illustrationOnLine.com.

Making a Thai Boxing Champion

Photography Credits:

TP © Maciej Tomczak/phototramp.com/Alamy, K6-7 © Jodi Cobb/National Geographic Image Collection, K10 © Ronald Macpherson/Alamy, K11 © Jodi Cobb/National Geographic Image Collection, K12-13 © Darby Sawchuk/Alamy, K14 © Maciej Tomczak/phototramp.com/Alamy, K15 © Brent Winebrenner/Lonely Planet Images, K16 © Darby Sawchuk/Alamy, K16-17 © Alan Howden-Muay Thai Stock/Alamy, K18 © Al Bello/Getty Images, K22-23 © PhotoDisc/CD-Colors-Signature Series, K23 © McPherson Colin/CORBIS SYGMA.

Illustration Credits:

K2 (t) © Mapping Specialists, Ltd. Madison, WI, USA, K2 (b), K3, K4-5, K8-9 © Phil Saunders/American Artists Rep., Inc.

Water Sports Adventure

Photography Credits:

TP © Darryl leniuk/Getty Images, L4-5 © Ryan Fox/lonely Planet Images, L6-7 © Ron Niebrugge/Alamy, L10 © PCL/Alamy, L10-11 © Darryl Leniuk/Getty Images, L12-13 © Joe Fox/Alamy, L16-17, © Ron Niebrugge/Alamy, L18 © Chris Willson/Alamy, L18-19 © Ethan Janson/Getty Images, L22 © PhotoDisc/CD-Nature, Wildlife and Environment, L23 © Michael Blann/Getty Images.

Illustration Credits:

L2 (t), © Mapping Specialists, Ltd. Madison, WI, USA, L2-3, L8-9, L14-15 © Patrick Gnan/illustrationOnLine.com.

Credits (continued)

Dinosaur Search

Photography Credits:
TP © Cardozo,Yvette/Alamy, M4 © TNT MAGAZINE/Alamy, M4-5 © Tibor Bognar/Alamy, M6-7 © Sergio Pitamitz/Getty Images, M8-9 © TNT MAGAZINE/Alamy, M10-11 © The Natural History Museum/Alamy, M12 © Philip Lewis/Alamy, M13 © The Natural History Museum/Alamy, M18-19 © Woodfall Wild Images/Alamy, M22-23 © PhotoDisc/CD-Backgrounds and Textures, M22 (b) © Sinclair Stammers/Photo Researchers, Inc., M23 © Alberto Paredes/Alamy.

Illustration Credits:
M2 (t) © Mapping Specialists, Ltd. Madison, WI, USA, M2-3, M14-15, M16-17 © Mark Gerber.

The Memory Man

Photography Credits:
TP © Arthur S. Aubry/Getty Images, N6-7 © Richard Mills/Lonely Planet Images, N7 © fStop/SuperStock, N8 © Elly Godfroy/Alamy, N9 © Arthur S. Aubry/Getty Images, N12 © Scenics & Science/Alamy, N13 © Stockbyte.Getty Images, N14-15 © Thomas Barwick/Getty Images, N16-17 © Index Stock/Alamy, N18-19 © Bill Aron/Photo Edit, N22-23 © Glow Images/Alamy.

Illustration Credits:
N2 (t) © Mapping Specialists, Ltd. Madison, WI, USA, N2-3, N4-5, N10-11 ©Sharon and Joel Harris/illustrationOnLine.com.

Wild Animal Trackers

Photography Credits:
TP © S Purdy Matthews/Getty Images, O4-5 © Frank Krahmer/Getty Images, O6-7 © Martin Norris/Alamy, O8 © Terry Whittaker/Photo Researchers, Inc., O8-9 © JOY TESSMAN/Getty Images, O10-11 © Heinrich van den Berg/Getty Images, O14-15 © Ed Kashi/Corbis, O18-19 © Mark Pearson/Alamy, O22 © Max Dannenbaum/Getty Images, O23 © John James/Alamy.

Illustration Credits:
O2 (t) © Mapping Specialists, Ltd. Madison, WI, USA, O2-3 © Roger Kent/illustrationweb.com, O12-13, O16-17 © Alan Baker/illustrationweb.com.